CW00458043

How To Recover From

Open Heart Surgery

Based on a true story by

Steve Corkhill

Published by FlatBear Publishing

PO Box 3679, Bath, UK. BA2 4WS

ISBN 978-1-910291-25-2

www.flatbear.net

Table of Contents

More Contents

This is a true story. Well, over 95% of it is. Just like the average global success rate of open heart surgery procedures.

All characters are real; all of the key events are real and in sequence; all feelings and emotions described were very real.

All names have been changed.

I hope that everybody who reads it will be both entertained and learn a lot about what to expect when either themselves or a loved one experiences this operation.

For the hundreds of thousands of people around the world who will find themselves in this position this year. Take comfort - it's not a lost cause by any means.

Chapter 1 – A New Day Dawns

*"A journey of a thousand miles begins
with one step." Lao Tzu*

Someone was nudging his right shoulder. "Time to wake
up, Benedict. Come on. Can you hear me?" Ben looked out
through a fuzzy fog at a pair of faces smiling at him.

"Ah, the first day of the rest of my life. It worked,
then," he thought dozily.

"He's coming round. Hello Benedict. Benedict? Can
you hear me?" said the nurse. Without waiting for an
answer, she moved into a well-practiced routine, checking
his eyeballs and looking for other signs to confirm that
things were roughly as they should be for a patient
straight after surgery.

He wasn't entirely sure where he was. On a trolley
somewhere. Hopefully still in hospital. His mouth felt dry
and his body felt chilly. He was vaguely aware of being
pinned down although he had a warm feeling of being in
competent hands. That was a good start.

"Good afternoon Benedict," grinned the big man with
the bald head. He recognised him as surgeon Massimo.

"The operation was a success. We managed to repair that leaky valve and stitched up the little hole in the heart you had. I'm pleased with how it went. Now all we need to do is get you better."

"You're in intensive care. You've been out for about eight hours so far. This is Polly" he said, introducing the nurse, "she will be looking after you for the next twenty four hours or so to make sure you get stable, then we'll move you to another ward."

"Hello Benedict" she smiled. "Here, let me take that tube out of your mouth. It's been helping you breathe while you were out. You should be OK to do that on your own now. Could you cough for me while I quickly pull it out, please?"

He gagged and coughed meekly as she gently tugged the tube out through his mouth. He was surprised how long it was. He was glad he wasn't awake when they tried to put that in.

"Hold this," Polly said and handed him a neatly rolled-up towel. "This is your new best friend. Hold it against your chest whenever you want to move. It will help protect your breastbone when you clear your throat or shift position. It forces your arms in close to your ribs. That limits movement so it doesn't hurt so much."

As she placed it on his chest, Ben noticed a large dressing and felt rather than saw other attachments. He already knew about the one in his right hand but there seemed to be a lot more going on. Mind you, he couldn't really be sure as he still felt really groggy. And chilly. Now she had mentioned it, he could feel his chest was a bit tight.

"Try to cough about five times every thirty minutes or so. It will help to clear your lungs," she said.

Ben clutched the towel to his chest and gave another feeble little cough followed by a tiny squeak as the movement gave a gentle tug at the stitches in his chest. His throat felt raw. "It's as if a big tube had been shoved down it and left for eight hours" he thought and inwardly smirked at his own wit.

"Yes, it probably feels a bit raw so it's likely to be a bit sore. But it's important to start breathing deeply as soon as you can so your lungs are cleared naturally."

Bit by bit Ben was becoming more aware of his surroundings. He vaguely remembered reading that the valve repair operation would include having a machine to do the breathing for him while he was under, so it was important he cleared his lungs now that he was back in the land of the living.

Polly grinned at his squeak. "That's a good sign, though. You're waking up. Now, you'll probably feel quite a few things attached to you. I'll just explain what they are for. They're all pretty standard."

Working from top to bottom, she pointed out the cannula in his neck, the thick dressing protecting his sternum, an unexpected pair of drainage tubes at the bottom of his chest, the cannula on his hand and a catheter in his penis. They were attached to a battery of machines on a trolley next to him, quietly bleeping away, apparently monitoring everything going on with his body. And he was wearing a pair of very tight, knee length, toeless white socks.

As he looked down he thought that whoever had managed to insert that catheter in such a chilly environment had done the equivalent of threading a camel through the eye of a needle. Very impressive. He grimaced at the thought of how that was done then once again grinned inwardly. He thought the socks looked ridiculous and decided that someone must have been heaving away at him to get them on at all.

"These nurses must be very strong. Crikey, I must have been really out of it," he thought. Then he moved his head to the side and felt a quiver of concern as he imagined the stitches in his chest tug once again. Surely there was no way they could pull apart, was there?

"Any questions? There's no rush. There will be someone with you all the time now until you move on."

There was only one possible question to come up with. Nothing to do with the people in the room, or whether

4

his wife Jamie knew he was awake, or the awesome array of high technology, or whether he was going to live. Oh, no. Nothing so clever.

"Could you call me Ben, please?" he said. "I only get called Benedict when I'm in trouble with my mother." At another time he would have added "Or the police," but even in his dopey state he realised that a little joke like that wouldn't have been appropriate for now. Not with these very serious people who had only recently had him laid out on a slab with his heart literally in their hands.

Everyone has irrational hatreds. Using 'Benedict' and having to give his date of birth were most certainly two of his. Two of a growing number, if the truth be known. But this was current and so it mattered.

He could just about accept Benedict being used in formal situations as it was on his birth certificate and thus on all of his important documents. The rest of the time, he truly loathed its use, particularly without his permission, and he really didn't need any more stress at the moment. It didn't matter that the stress would be self-inflicted, infantile and pathetic. No, he had open heart surgery to recover from and one way he would do that was to be called Ben and not Benedict. Capisce?

"Ok. I'll do that," she said with a smile. Ben felt rather than saw her roll her eyes at Massimo. Now that the key question of the moment had been answered, Massimo said that they would leave him to get on with things and withdrew from the small room.

He had expected to be sleeping and dreaming of fairies and unicorns for the first twenty hours or so, rather than feeling irrationally stressed about his name.

A few minutes later, after checking the screens, Polly got back to business.

"You may occasionally feel some pain. Here, hold this," she said, pushing a small tube into his right hand. "If you think you need any painkillers at any stage, press the button on the top. It will give you a small measure of morphine. Don't worry, it's controlled and won't reopen for five minutes after you've used it. You can't overdose."

Ben remembered his mate Simon telling him about his own operation. He had been just twenty one years old and on the cusp of a top sporting career. "The only bit of advice I'd offer is that when it comes to painkillers, don't be a hero. Use them. I didn't and I regretted it."

Simon had gone on to have a long career in first class sport after that, so it had given Ben confidence that a full recovery was possible. At a time when he had been struggling to get any specific answers from the medics about recovering from this operation, it meant that anything Simon said had immediate credibility. Ben especially liked the thought of not needing to be brave at first. Not that he would need it, of course. Oh no. But it was always going to be useful to have a fall-back option. Just in case.

Ben pressed the button. Felt nothing. Pressed it again, just to check what he had been told. He was a man, after all. It was in his genes to check. Felt nothing again. Maybe he was still anaesthetised.

He became aware that his back felt tight and remembered something that Charlie the anaesthetist had said the previous afternoon. Charlie said that opening the chest and moving the ribs apart would mean that there would be unusual stresses on his back as the rib cage was moved aside.

Of course. How obvious. Ben hadn't thought about that before, yet it was only basic mechanics.

As a result, Ben saw this discomfort as a plus. It was confirming his expectations and so was A Good Thing.

His last thought was to wonder whether everything would go as he hoped over the next few weeks. He had a plan. It would be nice if it all fell into place because then he would be back to his best in a month or two.

He pressed the button again and closed his eyes.

Chapter 2 – The Road To Destiny

"Expect the unexpected."

Precisely three hundred and thirty three days earlier, Ben had been enthusiastically helping his friend Stuart celebrate the news that he had been given the all clear from prostate cancer. There was a lot of wine involved and as the day progressed the conversation briefly turned to his own health.

He was feeling pretty good, he said. Fairly confident. Mind you, although he was exercising more and more each month, he could feel himself getting older.

"I feel like King Canute trying to stop the tide. It only seems to be slowing up the rate of decline rather than improving things," he grumbled.

He got breathless much more easily and it was getting to be a challenge to stride up the steep hill from town. In fact, a couple of times recently he had needed to stop halfway to get his breath back. Admittedly, both times were soon after a heavy gym session, so that was probably understandable. He was simply getting older and had to learn to accept it.

He also had a regular little cough and sometimes his acid reflux was a bit painful. Oh, and Jamie was going on about his breathing being erratic and shallow while he was asleep.

Stuart started banging on again.

"And you haven't had your prostate check yet, have you? Please do it. I couldn't recommend it highly enough for men of our age. It saved my life. Book it today. It's not a joke. Please get it done."

Ben promised he would, even if only to stop this focus on him. This was supposed to be Stuart's day.

Ben had a positive nature as a matter of choice, mainly because he preferred it to the miserable and negative alternative. It had proved time and again throughout his life to be the better approach.

His outlook was encapsulated in the phrases 'there's nothing you can't learn from' and 'you can find something positive in everything that happens'. He was also very aware that everybody's attitude influences people around them, which is often reflected in the way they are subsequently treated.

Attitude was also the one thing that was always his choice: nobody else could choose it. In that respect he felt he always had an element of control of what went on around him. It was never total because he knew that occasionally under stress he forgot to choose and reacted with instinct and emotion instead. That was always when trouble started although he still hadn't managed to master that simple fact.

Ben was good to his word and went for a check-up. When the doctor said he heard a small whoosh from his heart, he wasn't overly concerned. Yes he would go for another test. No problem. He had just been told that his prostate was fine anyway, so Yay!

He was still quite happy despite each subsequent test revealing that the problem was worse each time. "It'll be OK," he tried to assure Jamie as they waited for the next test. The fact that the wait between tests was so long implied to him that it couldn't be serious. They'd have him in straight away if it was. Surely?

There are many countries around the world where there is no real concept of a waiting list. Ben didn't live in one of those. In his country, there was a Process to be followed and that was that. The patient fits into the Process and not the other way round. It meant that he had to wait until the Process was ready. If it was full, well, he must wait until his turn.

First there was the twelve-lead electrocardiogram – an ECG – and it suggested that there was a potential issue needing further investigation, so he was sent to a specialist hospital for an echocardiogram. This showed that there was actually something wrong and it was a bit more than small. However, quite how much more than small wasn't clear, so he should get an even more accurate test. He would be put on a waiting list for a Trans-Oesophageal Echocardiogram, known internationally as a TEE.

Meanwhile, he was advised, it just may be worth completing any ongoing dental work because the gums were the easiest way for rogue viruses to enter the blood stream and potentially affect the heart. It may also be worth checking his eyesight. What was there to lose? He arranged for checks on his eyes and teeth, although it didn't help the growing concern at home when he found he needed some new spectacles and the dentist gave him his immediate and undivided attention.

The longer the wait for an appointment, the more convinced he was that this couldn't be anything serious. In his mind, a positive outlook would win out and eventually silence Jamie's concerns.

Jamie attended every discussion about these tests. Her deep and thorough medical knowledge was invaluable in catching the subtle implications of the jargon-filled sentences that were thrown at him.

The downside of course is that she was also aware of what could go wrong or what the implications of one decision over another could have. So naturally she had some informed concerns.

Ben, though, put it to the back of his mind and got on with his work. He was busy enough at work anyway, and was planning a major holiday for just the two of them in three months' time.

Eventually a date came and he went for his TEE.

This was a much more serious procedure that took up almost a full day. Rather than hanging around a waiting room as usual, this time he was allocated a temporary bed. The TEE was a physically uncomfortable experience and he didn't enjoy it, gagging on the device as it was eased down his throat despite the light sedation.

When the cardiologist reviewed the results and confirmed that actually, yes, there was an issue with his mitral valve and that it was serious, he started to think for the first time that this could be real. Then when she added that it was so serious that they should bypass the normal route and contact the cardiac surgeon directly, he actually felt a little nervous.

"He will be in contact with you very quickly to arrange an appointment," she promised. In the end, 'very quickly' meant two weeks, which gave him plenty of time to stew in his own thoughts. Stress and worry tussled with a determination to stay positive and find a way to make the best of things, regardless of how concerned he got. Most worrying was pointless anyway.

Ben was a firm believer in preparation. He wasn't keen on unpleasant surprises and always felt a lot more confident if he had an idea what was coming up. "Proper Prior Preparation Prevents P#ss Poor Performance" was one of his mantras that he used in all aspects of his life. He remembered being introduced to the phrase by quite possibly the least organised man he had ever worked with, a technical genius with wild hair and a manic look in his eyes. The memory always made him smile.

He started to look into what it could all mean. There was plenty of technical information available on the internet, which was probably as clear as a bell if he spoke Latin and was a practicing doctor. But he wasn't, and as a lay person it was a challenge to relate to it and to appreciate the implications.

He researched more and more although kept his knowledge and learnings to himself. This was for his information – just in case. Jamie seemed to be too keen to expect the worst possible outcome and he wasn't interested in talking about what would go wrong. He wanted to know what could go right.

Three questions dominated his thoughts: What will it mean for me? How long will I be out of action for? And is there anything I can do to speed it up? He had a major holiday to go on and as a self-employed person it was essential he could tell his clients when he would be off and for how long because that had a direct impact on his income. He wanted to know this information yet couldn't find it and nobody would tell him.

The more he researched, the more confusing it became and the further away from the answers he felt. Everything he looked at seemed to conclude that 'it depends' and didn't elaborate. It was frustrating as he now accepted that a procedure of some sort was probably going to be necessary and he wanted to know what to expect.

He did find a couple of notes where it was suggested that 'recovery could take four to six weeks' so he decided to use that as a starting point. Six weeks is a long time although he could still be on the flight in two months if everyone got a move on.

He presumed it would be uncomfortable, and he guessed he would probably end up with a big scar on his chest and become a member of the famed zipper club for veterans of this type of operation. He would do whatever he could do to make his recovery as rapid and complete as possible. Although he was getting a bit nervous, especially when he saw some of the graphic images on YouTube, he was still upbeat.

The word 'recovery' has different connotations for different people.

He decided he would define his recovery as being when he got back to the level of fitness and functionality he was at when this little issue had first been identified. That gave him an end goal. Some more digging unearthed the useful gem that mentioned that people could think of returning to light work after about eight weeks.

That was helpful. At least there was an idea now, even if eight weeks sounded like a ridiculously long time. Probably over-cautious. Nevertheless, he started to think in terms of being back firing on all cylinders in eight weeks. This was after all a new experience for him so he decided to allow for the maximum possible time and expect to be ready earlier. That was another of his little mantras – 'Plan for the worst and hope for the best'.

So – he would probably be out of work for about two months. The more he thought about it, that could be quite useful. It would certainly test his savings, but it would also give him a chance to catch up on a few personal projects that had long been on the back burner. He started to get a little excited at the prospect. Something positive could come out of this, so bring it on.

He started to think of things he would do to ensure he hit the eight-week mark for his recovery. There would be the physical bit and he knew that there would be a strong psychological element.

He would get as fit as possible beforehand, then spend the recovery time walking in the sunshine and countryside, doing activities that he knew he would enjoy and would bring a smile to his face in between his personal projects. A regular flow of the feel-good dopamine would do him more good than any drugs that could be prescribed. What had he heard? The brain contains the most powerful drug cabinet in the world? That sounded about right. He would tap into that.

He also knew that it would help to eat well. He already ate plenty of fresh food and cookies and sweets were limited to occasional binge sessions. All in all, he felt his own consumption wasn't too bad already, so there shouldn't need to be big changes. Yes, he was a bit overweight, but that was probably down to the beer and wine. He'd eat well and cut the booze down for the first six weeks. Shouldn't be difficult. That would surely help things along. He may even shed a few kilos while he was at it. That would be a nice little bonus.

He had the start of a plan, which was important in his world. A plan provided a big picture to focus on when things got awkward, which he knew was certain to happen. It would help to take away some of the fear and trepidation. With a plan he wouldn't be stepping into the unknown each day and he knew he could and would adjust it as time moved on and he found out more. 'Plan – Do – Review. Then repeat'. Yet another of his mantras.

Finally a date came through for an appointment to meet with a surgeon called Massimo. He felt prepared, whatever the outcome. He had done his homework and that had helped to keep a lid on his emotions. Today the positive attitude was winning, although he had to admit that the previous weekend the anxiety and fear of the unknown had really had him by the throat.

As he set off for his appointment he felt pretty good. He was fit for a man of his age and all in all felt cheerful and hearty. Whatever news this guy Massimo came out with couldn't be too bad, could it?

Yet when his name was called out his knees were shaking uncontrollably.

Chapter 3 – A High Impact Half Hour

*"A major life decision is never a choice but
rather a realisation that the decision
has already been made." Doug Cooper.*

So do you want to go ahead with an operation? You
probably should," said Massimo.

Eek.

That made it real. VERY real.

No more hiding behind faint hopes that it was all a
terrific misunderstanding or a mistaken identity that
would give him an entertaining story to tell for years
ahead. No chance.

At the start of the consultation he had felt that
generally things were OK. Now he felt the opposite.

It had been a very frank discussion with Massimo. On
the bright side, he was getting commentary that applied
specifically to him, rather than a generalised 'it depends'.
On the not-so-bright side, he now knew that something
really was wrong. And it wasn't good news.

Massimo had probed with a few questions and
identified a classic series of symptoms. Ben had

presumed that the breathlessness, the shallow breathing rate, the increased heart rate, the snoozing, slowing down and regular fatigue was all a part of his reluctantly getting older.

"It's not you getting older. You're ill."

Ben took in a long slow breath. Externally, he appeared calm and in control. Internally his mind was churning and he actually squinted as he tried to take the statement in. He could feel white coat syndrome crawling through his mind like a physical force that he was powerless to resist. So much for being in rational control of his emotions.

He had no idea what his mouth was saying. All he could hear was his mind screaming "This guy is a professor and he says I'm ILL. So I must be."

Up to now he had convinced himself that, if anything, he was merely damaged and damage could be repaired. ILL was different. ILL meant that a full recovery by his definition wasn't an option. ILL meant there could be more wrong. ILL probably also meant radical changes to lifestyle.

This was disastrous.

Meanwhile Massimo was still talking. He had considered the option to run some more tests by giving

Ben a chest monitor to wear for a time. However he believed that would only show what he already knew – there was a mitral valve leak that was at the top end of the severity scale and it had been getting worse over recent months. He also said there was a septal defect, which Jamie quickly translated as being a hole in the heart. A small one, but a hole nonetheless and Massimo added that it won't have been helping things, really.

"Everyone is born with one but it usually closes up. In some it doesn't and for many it goes unnoticed all their lives, so it's not major. It would be useful to fix them both at the same time though."

He had explained that the valve is a little bit like a parachute that gets pulled into place to prevent blood flowing back towards the lungs. "It's as if some of the strings have stopped working properly, so the valve can't close fully and the blood is pumped backwards rather than out into your arteries." Apparently a lot of it wasn't getting pumped in the right direction.

No wonder Ben got tired. His muscles were getting considerably less oxygenated blood than they needed. Exercising was actually making things worse because his heart was working harder and harder to provide less and less of a result.

The answer was easy. Those strings just need to be tightened up or reattached. Ideally reattached.

Massimo always preferred to repair a valve rather than replace it if at all possible and there was a pretty good chance that would be feasible. This was a bit of good news to hang on to.

If it was replaced there was a choice of either a man-made valve or one grown out of pig or cow tissue. Although the replacements were getting better all the time it would eventually wear out and the procedure would need to be repeated at some time about fifteen or twenty years in the future. And it would mean taking pills for the rest of his life and possibly a little clicking sound on each heartbeat.

If it could be repaired, he may well be sorted out in a one-off visit and there may not be any need to take pills other than aspirin. He'd have to take some for a few months while he recovered, sure. But not for life.

A repair was preferable although Massimo explained that it would be Ben's choice about which option to take if he decided to go for the operation.

And of course one of Ben's choices would be to ignore this conversation, walk away and take his chances. Although there is a success rate of well over 90% for these operations, there is still a small chance that things can go wrong.

In Massimo's opinion, though, his heart would probably fail by the end of the year and that could end up either being terminal or creating an emergency situation where the odds would be worse.

"So do you want to go ahead with an operation? You probably should."

He and Jamie exchanged looks. It was a complete and utter no-brainer.

Of course he should go ahead with it, and as soon as possible, please. The chances of anything going seriously wrong were very low and his own fitness would reduce those a bit more. It was either that or face the prospect of slowly becoming more and more inactive. Not an acceptable option, thanks.

Now he really did want to know how long he would be out of action, what was actually involved and what he could do to make it quicker or easier.

How hard could he exercise? He wanted to be as fit as possible going in to help his recovery.

And how soon can it be done? Will it be two weeks or three? He felt it was bound to be that close because they had been told that this was urgent, after all. He would have his work cut out to make sure he got his project into a position to hand it over in that time.

Massimo explained that everyone is different so he couldn't say how long he would be out of action other than "typically two or three months or maybe longer." The hospital would let him know the fine details of what to expect as the operation got closer. Meanwhile, just do moderate exercise if you must and get plenty of rest. Oh, and the waiting list for the operation was approximately twelve weeks.

"Twelve weeks?" Ben tried to keep the alarm out of his voice. That's three months. If he'd heard Massimo right, he could be dead by then.

The operation didn't worry him in the least. It was performed hundreds of thousands of times around the world each year; there are teams at this very hospital who do it every day of their working lives; there is a success rate of a long way over 90% and it's been getting done since 1928. There were no surprises to be had, so it was almost certain to be a success.

However the prospect of waiting for another three months did. No wonder it felt real. It was terrifying.

And what the f#ck was 'moderate' exercise?

Chapter 4 – The Pendulum Swings

*"Patience is not the ability to wait but the ability
to keep a good attitude while waiting."*

Joyce Meyer

Now that a well-known consultant had told him that he
was unwell, things felt very different.

The very first thing he had to do was cancel his long-
planned and already-paid-for holiday. He sincerely hoped
that the travel insurance would cover the cost, although
somehow doubted it.

The waiting that had previously merely irritated him
now started to prey on his mind because there was
now a potentially bad outcome from a delay, one that
would affect him. He tried to maintain a calm exterior
yet he couldn't ignore how the worry was affecting him,
especially when he hadn't heard anything six weeks after
the meeting other than the fact that he was "on a list."

The stress and frustration were building and he
couldn't even release the tension by using his preferred
method of doing something physically intense as that
could backfire on him.

He mentioned his situation only to a select handful of people who would be directly impacted when he was out of action. He couldn't say when it would start or how long it would last. All he could do was warn them that they would be affected at some point.

It was not knowing that was the problem. The uncertainty was hard.

He always felt comfortable when he thought he was being constructive. So he created a schedule of activities based on the estimate of a twelve-week wait. As well as working on his stamina and flexibility, he wanted to get work into a position where he could hand it over cleanly. He wanted to get his personal papers straight, too.

Getting his papers straight meant he could leave things tidy in the unlikely-but-still-possible scenario that it could all go wrong. It demanded that he at least think about the prospect. He was aware that that line of thought had the potential to lead him into some very dark areas and vowed to keep a tight rein on it.

He was conscious of the advice to do 'moderate' exercise, so he felt he needed to work for longer and longer to get any enjoyment or benefit.

That quickly started to take up a disproportionate amount of his time yet he felt he was still going downhill. He started to notice himself getting breathless more and more easily and he had to stop more often when walking up the hill from town.

He did wonder if that was purely psychosomatic and a direct result of just being told that he was ill. He concluded that it probably was, yet he still needed to stop halfway up the hill. He could feel the bar being lowered on his performance.

He had found two main definitions for 'moderate' exercise. The first was a basic calculation of an upper and lower limit for his heart rate and the second was considerably less scientific: work hard enough to be able to talk comfortably but not to sing.

Ben liked both numbers and singing. However, the previous Christmas Jamie had given him a snazzy wrist-based heart monitor to help with general training, so he opted for the basic calculation.

The simple method was to take his age off the number 220 and that provided him with a maximum heart rate. He should then work his heart within a range of 50% to 70% of that number. As he would turn sixty before too long he went with a maximum rate of 160, so his 'moderate exercise' range should be a heart rate of between 80 and 112.

It wasn't ideal, but it was more satisfying to work his brain a little rather than simply guess whether he would get breathless if he burst into song.

Professionally, his contracts effectively involved making his job redundant so the business he was working with could work smoothly without him. Although counter-intuitive to many, this usually worked well, as in doing so he would demonstrate that he was doing his job properly and, as a result, the business would frequently re-engage him elsewhere. He enjoyed the arrangement as it provided just enough pressure to keep him on his toes and ensure he was effective every day.

This was a different scenario. This time he couldn't yet say if or when he would next be around to be offered another role. It would be all too easy for the business to forget about him. As a self-employed person approaching the age of sixty this could easily have significant long term financial implications, and without a date or any idea of how long he would be out of action, there was nothing he could do to ease that situation. All he could do was make sure things were ready to be handed over smoothly when the time came and hope that he would not be forgotten.

This time the arrangement that gave him such a lot of job satisfaction was working against him.

Getting his papers straight left him feeling neat and organised, especially as this was always the chore that was pushed to the bottom of the pile as soon as anything more interesting came along. In the space of a week he updated and logged every relevant password and cancelled a load of aged and unnecessary memberships. It felt tidy. He had cleared a nagging issue and when he added the fact that his eyes and teeth had already had a thorough check, it gave him a real boost.

He was looking after the things that were under his control and it made him feel he was being constructive. That always helps.

He felt even better soon after when Jamie confirmed that the insurance company paid up for the abandoned holiday. They also discovered that had anything gone wrong while he was away he wouldn't have been covered. What an unexpected result. What a stroke of luck he'd been up for that check-up. He gave Jamie a high five and praised their good fortune.

Over a three-week period he pondered the question of "What if?" It was a simple yet incredibly stress-inducing question and he had to work hard not to get drawn into thinking about the possibilities. What if he died? What if something went terribly wrong and he didn't die? What if he had a stroke and was left unable to move? It was a dangerous path to start along and he had to force himself to focus on creating a place to start and not what it would mean if it happened. It was a close thing, though.

He was pleased that he could ask himself the questions and not get down. It made him feel strong. He identified and documented how to access all of the business and family finances and insurances and wrote a couple of letters to be opened in the event of a catastrophe. He even worked out the detail of what he would like in his own funeral. How maudlin. How encouraging. How powerful it was to think about his own eulogy. He vowed to do something about that when this was all over.

After eleven full weeks of waiting and as the tension and strain ratcheted upwards he was finally given a provisional date for his operation – for four weeks later. He felt sick.

On the positive side, it meant that he could hand over his work at a very convenient point in the project.

On the downside, it left him feeling irrelevant and small. His case had been defined as urgent, yet he still had to wait for fifteen weeks and there had only been two automated and highly impersonal contacts with him in all that time.

Inside, he was worried, tense, stressed and scared. Externally he was still bullish and determined that he would turn this into a positive experience. It would only be for about two months after all, assuming that internet information about people typically starting back to office-based work in eight weeks was fairly accurate.

That would mean about six weeks to recover from the operation - his initial finding - plus another couple to get fit and strong again.

It was the same for Jamie, except she was fully aware that the longer this wait went on the closer to complete heart failure he was getting.

Swings of emotion within a single day were by now standard. He was ill yet he appreciated how incredibly lucky he had been to be where he was now; he was surrounded by goodwill, yet he was lonely. There was nobody he could talk to about what he felt deep inside.

In the long wait, he worked on strategies that could help him to get up again as he knew he'd be down at times during the coming weeks and months. He practiced deep breathing and basic mindfulness by simply picking a sound, a sight or a smell and focusing on it for half a minute at a time. He experimented with colours, clothing, teased his sense of smell, wondered at nature, worked on his posture... anything that would distract him or help him to reassert some degree of control over his nerves and concerns. Whether it worked or not was irrelevant. He enjoyed exploring and playing with ideas and they were a constructive alternative to allowing the concern about what could go wrong to invade his mind.

He was still trying to establish how long he was likely be out of action. He had found out exactly what went on during the operation and started to wonder whether a six week 'recovery' was realistic. Surely a bone as big as his sternum won't be fully repaired inside six weeks? It seemed to contradict the general knowledge he had picked up years before that a big bone can take twelve weeks to heal.

He should be able to drive after four weeks, so maybe it would be. It's a strong bone and they'd tie it up tight, wouldn't they? Maybe that helped to accelerate the recovery? He still couldn't get anyone to commit to anything other than 'it depends'.

He had been in hospital just twice before, both for injuries to his cheekbones after clashes on the sports field. In those cases he had only been in hospital for two days and had returned to work within four. Yet then the instruction had been clear: no contact sport for six weeks to give the tiny bone a chance to heal properly. Maybe his sternum would be well on the way to full repair after six weeks too? Enough to drive and survive an impact, no doubt. He'd work with that.

He was surprised to discover how many people had had direct experience of heart surgery. Many had either had a similar operation or knew someone close to them who had. Unfortunately, none could remember how long they had been out of action. The only bonus was that all of them survived.

So in the absence of advice to the contrary, he went with the eight week target to be back at work.

In the final four weeks of waiting he felt himself going downhill. Jamie knew he was getting close to heart failure. He had a deep fear of becoming old and immobile and he could feel himself sliding inexorably in that direction. He put on weight, his breathlessness increased and his skin changed tone. He was ill. He had been told so. He was starting to look the part.

He was booked in for a coronary angiogram, which is the best test for evaluating coronary artery disease. The surgeon would use it to identify precisely if there was anything else that needed doing while he was in there. The procedure would identify whether any of the blood vessels feeding his heart were blocked, in which case a bypass would be necessary. Much better to do all the work at the same time rather than have to repeat the procedure some time later, he was told. A rather bizarre 'two for the price of one' he'd prefer to do without.

It was a marvellous experience.

He loved the mass of technology focused solely on him and wondered at the skills of the person who deftly threaded a thin tube through his wrist up to his heart. He was encouraged to watch the screen that showed the action and was fascinated as he watched the dye being injected through the tube.

Then came the good news. The liquid flowed easily.

That meant there was no blockage.

That meant he wouldn't need a bypass.

And THAT meant he wasn't ill – he was just flawed.

And flaws can be fixed.

That changed everything.

These surgeons were basically super skilled mechanics who perform this surgery day in, day out over years. He was absolutely confident in their ability to sort out his errant valve and now he knew he was merely damaged and that there was no heart disease. It meant that a full recovery was a possibility.

What fantastic, fantastic news. He could look forward to this whole experience now. His grin made his jaw hurt.

The pendulum had swung back in his direction.

Chapter 5 – Final Preparations

"Things go up and down. If you can survive the down it will come back." John Denver

The final two weeks before the operation were hectic enough to distract him from thinking about the detail of what was about to happen.

He was called in for a pre-op meeting where he was taken through the logistics of what he should expect.

He was told that people with his condition should usually expect to be in hospital for between five and eight days. He would be encouraged to move and walk from the very start and to rest as much as possible. When home, he should gradually build up his stamina and make sure he took it slowly.

What was essential, though, was that he took responsibility for his own health. Sometimes it could get quite tough although nobody else would be able to do it for him. He had to do it himself.

If he took responsibility and obeyed instructions, he could make a decent recovery quite quickly; if not, it could take a lot longer.

"How quickly?"

"It depends."

Arghhh.

No mention was made of nutrition.

It would have made a big difference if it had been. Simple things like "drink two litres of water a day", "replace foods that have been processed or contain extra sugar or salt with natural foods wherever possible" and "sleep as much as you can". It was a missed opportunity.

A rough plan was starting to take shape. A week in hospital, another week to recover, then four weeks to restore movement and some fitness. Finally he would allow another two weeks to work on his stamina and get ready to go back to work, firing on all cylinders.

He liked to keep his mind busy and imagined that waiting around for eight weeks would mean he would have plenty of time to fill. He added more to the list of small projects he wanted to complete.

He prepared his hospital bag well in advance. He added a pair of front opening pyjamas, a dressing gown, slippers and his spectacles. He bought some colourful short sleeved shirts that would cheer him up when he wore them then added some shorts, a large sudoku magazine, three notebooks and he topped up his Kindle with a dozen books he now expected he would have plenty of time to read.

He had his last day at work with the project in a good place and with sympathetic instructions to come back when he could, although he was not to rush it. "If it's eight weeks, that's fine. If it's longer, that's fine too. Just get better." That gave him a bit of confidence that he wouldn't be discarded quite as easily as he had feared. It made him feel good.

Finally, a telephone call confirmed the date, although he was warned that he may be bounced as there were only a limited number of intensive care beds. He would be the first one in the list for that day, so he should see the anaesthetist in the afternoon before then check into the hospital in the evening.

The day before the operation, he met with Charlie the anaesthetist. Charlie made two powerful comments of striking interest.

The first was "Enjoy yourself this evening. It will be six weeks of hard and sustained effort before you feel like you do now."

"Six weeks?" thought Ben. "Suits me. I don't feel too bad right now so if I feel like this in six weeks that works. Even better, it's in line with my thinking so far. That's nice to know I was on the right track. I'll be comfortably back in work in eight weeks."

"Then," Charlie continued, "if all goes well, it will be about twelve weeks before you're even ready to start to fire on all cylinders again. Remember that. You need to apply yourself consistently for twelve weeks and only then will you be good to go. And that means you will be ready to start, not fully up and running and taking on the world as if nothing has happened. Certainly nothing like a press-up before then."

"It's vital you understand that you only have one shot at your breastbone healing, so you really do need to take it seriously. And if you don't, you'll run the risk of it not knitting together properly and that will give you a lifetime of problems. It's not worth it. For the sake of twelve weeks, do yourself a big favour. It's not a long time in the grand scheme of things. This isn't a race. In fact the slower you can make it, the better it will be for you in the long term."

Ben felt disappointed. Twelve weeks was a lot longer than he had in mind.

"Don't sulk," he told himself. "Charlie is the only one who has given any sort of answer to that question even if it doesn't fit with what I was hoping. Probably being over-cautious. Respect the experience and the honesty and ask how it can be made to happen earlier."

"What can I do to speed that up?"

"Realistically? You can't. Unless you can suddenly lose forty years in age and even then it could only be a week or so sooner. Honestly, your best bet will be to knuckle down, apply yourself and let nature do its work. And don't lift anything heavier than a mug of water for the first six full weeks."

The advice was unequivocal. Think in terms of twelve weeks. He could still target being back at work at around eight weeks but it was being made pretty clear that this recovery was going to take a lot longer than he had originally hoped. He felt restraints were being put on him. He needed to reset his mind and his expectations.

That evening Jamie and he went out for a meal. It was full of unspoken tension. He wanted to get on with it. She was dreading tomorrow.

After the meal she dropped him at the hospital entrance and reminded him not to get irritated about his name and date of birth. "It's perfectly valid and reasonable. They need it to identify you accurately."

He strode through the doors, mildly peeved at being chastised at his moment of imagined bravery. He was disappointed at the twelve weeks comment that afternoon, yet still confident in the outcome. He was

39

damaged, not ill. Damage can be fixed. He'd have to put up with some discomfort for a couple of months and then he could build himself back up. He had a plan and a focus. He just had to take things one step at a time

He would be the perfect patient - helpful, willing, accommodating and considerate.

As he walked through the door Jamie was watching him through the rear view mirror.

This was one of the worst moments of her life. She had no idea whether she would ever see him again.

Chapter 6 – Checking In

*"Every great move forward in your life begins
with a leap of faith, a step into the unknown."*
Brian Tracy

He was expected. On arrival he had to sign disclaimer forms, confirm that he was aware of the risks inherent with the procedure, hand over his belongings for security and get ready for bed. He could have a glass of water before midnight but then that was it. Nothing else.

"It's happening. No going back now. And it's a bit scarier than I had expected," he admitted.

At about ten p.m. along came a nurse called Grace, offering a small tablet to help him sleep once he had answered one or two questions.

"Date of birth?" she asked. Loudly enough for the next ward to hear.

He bristled. He hadn't lasted long.

"They're not even interested in my name. I'm a number already," he thought sulkily before mumbling his date of birth. He hated saying it aloud because, frankly, it

41

made him feel ancient, and he didn't have any desire whatsoever to feel any older than he already did.

"Name?"

"Ben. Not Benedict. Please call me Ben."

"Certainly," she said. "Ben it is," and she wrote it on a whiteboard above the bed. She fitted a cannula to the back of his right hand.

"Now for a slightly delicate question. Have your bowels moved today? And which of these was it most like?" With a flourish and a smile she pulled out a chart with seven pictures of turds varying in consistency.

Urgh. Ben was jolted into the present faster than the speed of light. He had presumed that he would have some moments that would rattle his sense of dignity · while he was in hospital, but this was like driving a herd of buffalo all over any notions of privacy within an hour of getting there. He blushed.

"Seriously?" he thought. "Blushing in front of this nurse who does this every day? Get over yourself."

Yet he felt his sense of privacy evaporating as he grunted "Yes, about ten hours ago," and pointed towards picture number four. Grace wrote it down and smiled. If that was meant to comfort him, it didn't work.

"Yes, that surprises most people when they come in here. It's important information for us though." He knew she was being friendly to help him feel at ease, yet with

42

each word he was starting to feel more like an object. He felt he was getting stripped naked bit by bit.

He took his tablet and drank the small glass of water. Then he lay down, read a little and fell asleep.

The following morning he was gently woken and instructed to shower and scrub every part of his body with a powerful antiseptic soap. He was given the classic hospital gown to wear and told to get back on his bed when he was ready.

The open back made him feel almost naked, which made him feel uncomfortable. "So ends any chance of impressing these people with my sartorial elegance," he thought, either drily or wittily – he wasn't sure which.

He wondered why they needed his back to be open when they're going to cut through his chest. He liked to pose rhetorical questions like that. It amused him. And it stopped him feeling quite so insignificant.

He was wheeled through long corridors towards the theatre. He felt mildly important as the temporary centre of attention until he passed a trolley being pushed in the opposite direction. The patient looked so unbelievably ill it made him feel a bit of a fraud.

Within fifteen minutes of gliding into the preparation room, his chest, arms and legs had been shaved and more items were connected to him. A heart monitor using sticky pads on his chest; a peg on his middle finger to monitor the oxygen in his blood and a drip linked in to the cannula on his hand.

Then he lay back and the theatre anaesthetist appeared upside down in his view.

"How are you feeling?" she said.

"Nervous."

She smiled.

"Think of your happy place and count backwards from one hundred."

He got to ninety seven.

Chapter 7 – Grim Days

"Keep calm and carry on." "This too shall pass."

Ben woke again. He looked at Polly's back as she busied herself at the screens. He tried making small talk but he was too dull-witted and she was busy.

What he wanted at that time was someone to talk to him, hold his hand and tell him he's doing OK. What he got was world class medical care. The magnificent array of technology was checking everything about his body, monitoring carefully against well-established norms.

Even in his befuddled state it struck him that he was merely the latest incumbent of that bed, identified by the combination of date of birth and his formal name. 'Ben' didn't matter to this environment. His body was getting the very best that medicine could offer and the medical staff would be measured on that. His mind was left to look after itself.

He consoled himself with the thought that of the thousands of people around the world who were at that instant sharing his exact situation, the vast majority would probably be feeling the same. Their bodies were being nursed through the delicate post-operative phase and their minds and spirits would need to follow in due course. Another mantra. "This too shall pass," he said to himself, determined not to sulk or feel down. It would only be for a short time.

But it would have been lovely for someone to tell him that he was doing OK.

The traditional open heart operation involves the breastbone being cracked open from top to bottom. A cardiopulmonary bypass machine is attached and the heart is chilled to help it to stop. Then the surgical team perform the intricate repairs required. Or, as Ben tended to describe it, the surgeon will have a good old rummage around and do whatever he finds needs to be done; repair, replace, remove or bypass. In some of the more extreme cases, all four.

A small hole in the internal walls of the heart is common, so this is closed off with a quick stitch or two. If a bypass is required, a blood vessel is taken out of the leg, arm or chest wall and used to bypass the damaged artery supplying the heart.

After all of this is done the heart is warmed up and restarted, the bypass machine disconnected and the sternum wired together. Finally the chest is stitched up and the patient wheeled to the intensive care ward for one-to-one care. Usually it's all finished in between two and three hours.

It was no real surprise that he felt a bit battered, or that the heart suffers peripheral damage in a large minority of operations. In most cases this only means a slightly longer and more complex post-op treatment, although in extreme cases it can get as bad as having to repeat the procedure.

Ben was aware of that before he went in. Now he was out and in intensive care he was wary of moving much, mainly because it could hurt and subconsciously he was concerned about disturbing the stitches deep inside his chest. The external ones were fine – it was the internal ones that made him fret.

He had been told to try to take at least five deep breaths every thirty minutes and to cough to help clear his lungs. They had been kept inflated by machine during the operation so needed to be brought back into action and cleared of any mucus.

Despite his mantra and desire to just let things follow their course, Ben drifted in and out of self-pity. His whole body felt sore; his chest, his back, his sides and even his ankle because the compression socks felt so tight. Already, merely hours into his recuperation, he really wanted someone to talk to who seemed to care about him. Someone who understood that he felt sore and lonely and scared. It wasn't coming from Polly so he took another shot of morphine. He tried to break the wait down into fifteen minute intervals. Time dragged.

Every time he suspected that he may soon feel pain, he would press his button. "Don't be brave," leapt into his mind each time so he happily pushed. He didn't know if he was getting relief, as even though he felt sore all over, he knew he wasn't hurting too much. "This too shall pass," he muttered to himself, breathing as deeply as he felt he could without causing a tug on the stitches. By breathing deeply he felt he was already contributing something to his recovery.

"Most people aren't sick from the drugs," they had told him. Oh, really?

He was. And how.

His two previous overnight stays in hospital had both resulted in spectacular vomits. "This time will be different", he had thought. His body had different ideas.

He threw up eight times during his short stay in intensive care. It was horrible. He felt nauseous and sore. Despite holding his rolled-up towel tight to his chest, he was too wary, scared or weak to perform a quick half roll in bed as he was terrified that he could pull the internal stitches apart and that Massimo would have to start all over again. Instead all he could do was turn his head to one side and unload, then put up with the feeling of the vomit oozing over his shoulder and down his neck.

"There goes another mouthful of dignity."

The first couple of times, an efficient cleansing wipe by an attentive Polly was all that was required. It was a joy to get a face wash at the perfect temperature. He felt clean, fresh and once again filled with hope that this experience would be over soon.

The fourth time, in the middle of the night, tired, confused and sore, he unloaded twice in rapid succession. A quick wipe wouldn't be enough to sort that out. It needed a bed bath. He had time to wonder where on earth it could all come from before feeling nauseous again and he closed his eyes tight like any good three year old would do.

Two tiny nurses appeared with what sounded like a mop, a bucket and a rubber blanket. Their black uniforms made them look like ninjas on a mission. They instructed him to roll over. It wasn't a request.

Clutching his towel tube tightly, he gingerly rolled over while they expertly slipped the rubber blanket under him. He was keen to avoid snagging any of the spaghetti of tubes going in and out of him; they were focussed on moving him around easily. Any last vestiges of dignity were abandoned as they wiped and sloshed out every orifice and crevasse. He flopped around on the bed like a fish on a pier, following instructions to hold his chest tight, breathe deep or to roll over again.

In his hapless state he started to think that he needed to accept that he really was a bit of a control freak. All he had to do was abandon himself to their care, and he couldn't. Then he wondered "What an odd thought to have at this time," and promptly fell asleep.

Twelve hours later he was moved from the single bedded intensive care to a larger High Dependency Unit ward. The morphine had been replaced with an alternative and he had already been out of bed for a couple of hours, sitting then walking on the spot to get his body moving again. Although it was limited he was delighted to feel he was getting mobile so soon.

He was moved ten metres to the new ward and he felt a little skip in his spirits. It was the next step and represented a movement forward. He had survived the operation and he was on his way!

As he was wheeled into the ward Dawn welcomed him with a cheery "Hello Benedict. What's your date of birth?"

"It's f#cking Ben," he muttered to himself as all self-congratulation and memories of progress evaporated.

Chapter 8 – The Cardiac Crew

*"The finest of pleasures are always the
unexpected ones."*

Moving to HDU meant joining a group where everyone knows what each other has been through and so tends to ooze with empathy.

Weak waves and nods across the ward greeted him, although he guessed that as he only expected to be here for a day or two, it wasn't too likely that he'd have an opportunity for any deep conversations with anyone. Besides, he felt rough and just wanted to wallow in his own cave with nobody bothering him.

"I'm the ward sister and we'll be looking after you. If you need to know anything, just ask," said Dawn.

"Could you please call me Ben? I know it's not major really, but it is to me at the moment."

"Of course. Not a problem," and she wrote it on the whiteboard above his bed.

"It's that easy?" he said.

"Yes."

"So why can't everyone effing well do that" he

chuntered to himself, then out loud said "How long before I can start exercising again?"

"That depends," she smiled. He closed his eyes in frustration. This was getting boring.

"Let's get you out of here first. You've had a big operation and need to recover from that. Then you can recuperate and start to heal. You'll get your drugs at the start and end of each day and we'll take bloods each morning.

We want you to get up and about as much as you can while you're here. Ideally you'll sit out of bed for about six hours today. Tomorrow you can get dressed in your normal clothes if you feel up to it. Now, have your bowels moved yet?"

He felt they really ought to know that, what with all the machinery that had been attached to him for the last day, then thought better of saying so.

The first day passed slowly. He tried to read yet couldn't concentrate. He tried his Sudoku puzzles and couldn't even complete an easy one. He tried to listen to music on his iPod but it was too easy to tangle up with the mix of wires and tubes. Urgh. It was slow.

He tried to lie down but his back hurt and he struggled to even breathe. He tried to sit up on the raised bed and he slid down the sheets. And on top of everything he was really sore. What a drag.

There were two high points that afternoon. First, Jamie appeared alongside his bed, having been advised to stay away for the first day while he was in intensive care. At last, a friendly face to moan at. Second, he worked out a way to get in and out of bed without any assistance. It was a long and slow process but it meant he could get himself back up the bed after he had slid down. Of course, it wasn't a case of simply pushing himself up. That wasn't permitted as it would put far too much strain on the stitches.

One step at a time.

In the middle of that night Ben woke up shivering. Whatever he did, he couldn't get warm. Extra blankets didn't work and, although he very carefully curled into a tight ball and hid and hugged his knees under the covers, he just got colder. Even closing his eyes really tightly didn't work as it had done when he was three years old.

At the same time as his teeth were chattering, the sweat seemed to be pouring out of him. He got scared. His breathing got shallower and any time he tried to draw in a deep breath his chest and ribs hurt more. Crying silent tears he muttered his mantra "This too shall pass" over and over.

He was shivering uncontrollably and in increasing pain. He felt completely alone even though there was a full complement of nursing staff and a room full of other patients around him. Sleep was impossible. He felt like he was in hell and he hated it.

After two very long hours, the shivering eased so his body could relax fractionally. That in turn let him inhale more deeply, and slowly he started to feel as normal as anyone thirty six hours after open heart surgery could reasonably feel.

He felt miserable. Desperately tired, he begged in vain for a sleeping tablet from the night nurse. She refused, saying that there was a chance it could react with whatever had caused his shivering in the first case. He slept fitfully for a maximum of thirty minutes at a time for the rest of the night.

Three hours later he was woken up. "Ben. What's your date of birth? Time for your tablets. There's a sleeping tablet in with this lot." He decided he needed different swearwords. The current lot weren't working.

Breakfast of sorts was delivered by a walking surly attitude called Iain. In casting a dirty plate on to the bedside table he demonstrated a natural mastery of body language that implied - no, yelled - that he really didn't want to be there. Once Ben had manoeuvred himself into a position to reach it, he ate it hungrily. It turned out that he was the only one on the ward who could, such was the unique taste. The same joyous experience came with lunch, only then there was an even greater volume of slop to be returned.

Much of his day was spent alternating between trying to read a little, trying a new puzzle, standing up, sitting down, closing his eyes. He was restless and he was tired. He had tried to sleep but it was impossible. The general hubbub of a hospital, the constant bleeping of monitors and the regular flow of visitors to others in the ward were enough to prevent that. Anyway, his back was getting stiffer and was dominating any other sensation.

The nurses concluded that his night time terrors had been the result of coming down off morphine. It wasn't unusual and the best thing to do had been to let it work its way through. Ben was horrified that he had such a strong reaction after just two days' use. What must it be like for drug addicts? It didn't bear thinking about and he felt a surge of sympathy.

Short conversations started up with his immediate neighbours. Everyone was in a similar boat and even though they had never met before, the common experience brought them together quickly. Within a couple of hours they had shared backgrounds and were chatting away as if they had been friends for years. Ben was struck by the intensity of his feelings at that point.

Starting to talk and getting a response had taken the edge off his loneliness.

Yes, he was tired. And yes, he had felt terrified and completely alone just twelve hours before. Yet now the feelings of closeness towards his new friends was extraordinarily moving.

Ben had always enjoyed the multiple aspects and ages of his personality. He was a strong, determined, organised and controlled professional, perpetually striving for excellence in all that he did. He was also the eleven year old boy who took delight in little things like finding a four leaf clover, skimming stones and inventing games for everything. And he was thoroughly enjoying turning into the grumpy old man for whom all things modern were either things of wonder or contributed to the terrible breakdown of a civilised society where gentlemen never wore hats indoors and comedians on television could do a whole sketch without effing and blinding or taking a snide swipe at somebody not in a position to defend themselves. He loved it all because each was a perfectly recognisable persona that could appear at any time. They made him laugh at himself, which provided him with a secret source of comfort when things got challenging in life.

He ignored the three year old that sometimes appeared as a different persona when he wanted to throw his toys out of the pram over some trivial matter. And it was always trivial.

Now he seemed to be in a room full of similar characters even though there was an age spread of over thirty years and a huge diversity of backgrounds. So in between feeling rough and sorry for himself, Ben had moments of extraordinary warmth. Once again, he felt the emotional roller-coaster in operation and realised that right now he should enjoy this bit.

Progress. Even if only a tiny step, it was still a step.

The rolled-up towel was something they all had in common. By now everyone had mastered the art of getting in and out of bed and moving around although gravity ensured that the big guy opposite continually slid down his bed. Visitors came and went, meals arrived and were returned and interests were shared.

Ben and three others were consistent and chatty occupants of the HDU. Ben's son named them the Cardiac Crew. The other beds tended to have a steady turnover of people, passing through either on their way towards or away from recovery. There were a few women among "the temporaries," as they were known.

Bree spent less than a day there, skipping through because she had been fabulously fit before her own operation. She had prepared properly and really looked after herself. It wasn't her fault that the waiting caused her heart to deteriorate so much that instead of a valve repair she had ended up requiring a lot more work. She was so fit that she passed rapidly through and went to the wards almost before they could interrogate her about her story.

Flo – "not bloody Florence" – was a glamorous and gloriously potty-mouthed woman who stayed overnight for observation after she had had a couple of stents installed. Staying in HDU was unusual for that procedure, although she was glad to receive the attention. In her case she had keeled over with a heart attack immediately after a gentle exercise class. She hooted at the irony and said that she couldn't wait to get out and enjoy the moments that she might have missed if the attack had taken her away.

And then there was Dennis. Such an arrogant man. He was uncouth, rude and didn't seem to accept that any rules applied to him, especially when requested by nursing staff. He was a political activist who had an opinion on everything and wouldn't hear any other. All rights without responsibility. He infuriated everyone.

"They" were out to get him, he reckoned. If "They" were the Cardiac Crew, he was pretty darned close to the truth. They were pleased when he was moved to a single ward quickly. Good riddance, Dennis. He had introduced an unsettling atmosphere just when their spirits had started to settle down.

Of the regular inhabitants, Ben was humbled by Veda's patience and self-control. He was a trim man with film-star good looks who had been in his hospital bed for four weeks just waiting for his operation. Ben was already itching to get out and he'd only been there a couple of days. Four weeks was an unimaginably long time.

Veda's operation had been postponed twice before it actually went ahead. Even now it was unclear whether it had been a success and there was a chance of even more work being required. Yet he still lay down patiently in his bed, calmly waiting for the next piece of news.

"Great name," said Ben. "Where did it come from? What does it mean?"

"Well, my mother went on the hippy trail to India after the Beatles made it popular then she got pregnant. Liked the idea of a kid named after the sacred texts of the Hindus. Thought all that lore and knowledge around the commune or wherever she was at the time would make us all blessed. Doesn't feel like that right now."

"You carry it well."

Veda came alive when he talked about the thrill of breeding and racing his birds, the peace found in fishing on the riverbank or the satisfaction of mending broken machines in his workshop. He was a man who liked to be busy so Ben was even more impressed by his ability to handle his impatience. "Well, what's the option? Get stressed and frustrated? It will happen when it happens and I'll get on with it from there" he would say.

In contrast, Clark Joseph Kent – "Yes, really," – reminded Ben of the literary character Jack Reacher. He was a giant of a man who seemed to measure two metres in every direction and weighed in at about 140 kilograms. He was also hilarious, eternally chirpy and outgoing, addicted to social media.

"Lucky for my old mam I turned out like Superman, innit?" he said. "And guess what? You'll never believe this. My missus is called Louise."

He had many and varied roles including running his own business getting rid of vermin, and working as a night club bouncer, basically doing the same thing by night as in day although with a slightly lesser nod to the law. "I punch first then ask questions later," he said as he described his antics. "Then I use my natural charm to deflect any follow-up." There followed a short discussion about whether Clark wanted a short term contract to eliminate Dennis.

Like Veda in the next bed to him, Clark was a bird man, wandering the hills and fields close to home, training his hawks and other birds of prey like an Arabian sheikh. He was there because he had had a massive heart attack, although had been completely unaware of it for days afterwards.

Kelvin had finally been stopped in his tracks by his developing condition. A week before, he had experienced the very real trauma of actually being in the anaesthetist's room getting prepared for his operation when it was bounced. Ben ventured that that could only possibly play on his mind.

"No not really. It's done now anyway, so it was all OK in the end. Nothing to worry about."

Another saint for Ben to admire and learn from.

Kelvin had taken early retirement from a nicely profitable specialty building business over twenty years earlier and had settled into a lovely life in the countryside. Except one day his condition climbed on his back and he slowed down to a point of almost zero activity. Now he was hopeful of being able to settle into a much more active retirement.

Ben, Veda, Clark and Kelvin. They made an interesting group and each would give and receive support from each other through sheer instinct. It was priceless. Impossible to value. Yet totally natural.

Bert was on the edge of this little group, sitting gnome-like on a chair next to his bed with his eyes locked on some future day when he could return to his beloved Elsie, occasionally chipping in to conversations with a gem of a comment.

Bert was the embodiment of the word 'stoic'. He had been employed by only one company in his life and had recently retired after sixty three years' service, shortly after his 60th wedding anniversary. And he never did even a single hour of overtime. "Mind," he added, "I never had a day sick nor clocked off a minute early neither. That's how I was brought up and that's how I ended."

Bert did silence spectacularly well and they decided that he rationed the number of words he used per day and that once they were used up, well, that was it.

Bert would sit and listen then smile with a twinkle in his eye and say nothing.

Chapter 9 – Laughter and Tears

"Life is a blend of laughter and tears, a combination of rain and sunshine."

Norman Vincent Peale

Before long, their misfortunes were turned into a game. Ben's valve repair was apparently trumped by Clark's double bypass; that in turn was beaten by Bert's double bypass with a raise of a pair of valve replacements. They couldn't decide whether Kelvin's triple bypass was a bigger operation.

Ben countered that physically opening up the heart and having a good dig around was bigger than simply pinning a new vessel or two to the outside. He reckoned that the bypass brigade were lightweights as all they had was an incision in their chests and a bit of a cut on their legs. They countered that that meant they had actually been properly ill and not simply in need of a little mechanical tightening up.

They all agreed that Veda's combination of double bypass, valve replacement, valve repair plus possible pacemaker won the Operation Of The Week award. Bert got second place because he was Bert. He smiled silently.

At times the group would be chatting easily, then at others it would drop into silence as each either gave in to fatigue or needed a rest from the effort of conversation.

At one point the room dropped into one of these silences as everyone pondered their fates, enjoyed the warmth of new friendships and tried to think of new anecdotes they could share that the others could appreciate.

And in the silence, Clark farted.

The sound of someone farting for some reason makes people the world over snigger and laugh – especially eleven year old boys. Quite why is unfathomable. Yet generations of comedians have built their acts on it the world over.

There was a communal intake of breath and for half a second there was silence. Then Veda snorted. Half a second later everyone guffawed. And half a second after that everyone yelled "Aaargh!" as they squashed their towels into their chests to protect them.

There followed two minutes of "Hah-Aaargh" while everyone tried to control it. The pain was bad…. But Clark had farted! Hah-Aaarrrggghh!!! Tears of laughter flowed alongside grimaces of pain. It was a group release of the tensions and concerns of the last few days.

Thereafter anything that even had the slightest potential of the hint of a trace of a funny side was pounced on as quickly as possible. Laughter is the best medicine after all. And how it hurt.

And of course it meant that Clark could tell the nurses that yes, his bowels had moved that day. He had won that particular race.

The moments of laughter and the intense closeness were matched by fatigue and frustration. In the ward rounds, the clinical team would stand at the end of their beds and talk in a huddle without sharing the discussion with them.

Ben thought it was just another example of him getting worked up for no reason yet soon found out that everybody felt annoyed. All of the staff seemed to be working incredibly hard and carried stressed looks on their faces and important looking notepads, yet the findings weren't being relayed to the people in the beds.

The problem with emotions is that they can appear out of nowhere for no reason at any time and sometimes it can be really difficult to control them when they arrive. Their intensity and variability was a bit of a shock to Ben and while he had prepared himself to expect ups and downs, it was the extremes that surprised him most.

He had expected to feel battered and bruised although wasn't quite prepared for this level of soreness and stiffness. Especially in his back.

Sleeping tablets only seemed to give any of them a maximum of an hour's rest before they wore off and left them feeling more tired than before. And they all agreed that nobody had warned them it would hurt so much to simply breathe in and out.

He was tired, stiff and sore and was being excluded from the clinical conversations that he knew were about him. Out went the calm and rational reasoning of his professional persona and in stepped the hyper-sensitive three year old driven by emotion.

He started to rail to himself about the Process. He felt like he was just another lump of flesh. 'Stuff' would happen and he would be spat out at the end, physically fixed enough to allow the bed to be vacated before the next lump of flesh was rolled in.

The problem was that he was Ben, not simply a body or 'the patient' or 'bed 6'. Oh my goodness, how it irked him. And didn't he go on about it to Jamie when she came in to visit each day. Fortunately she was a very patient listener.

In a small way, that was a relief to her. She was finding the whole experience to be draining and terrifying. She too felt completely out of control as there was absolutely nothing she could do. She held a secret fear that the big heart of the man she had married almost thirty five years before may in some way be damaged. There was no logic to it, yet that's the way she felt. And to top it all off, as well as trying to hold it together for Ben and herself, she was also trying to support and encourage the rest of their family.

Ben didn't realise how many people he loved were being affected by his experience.

 Following the operation Ben had developed an atrial flutter – an irregular heartbeat and a mild version of atrial fibrillation – and he was being held in the HDU to see if drugs could sort it out. He was now bored as well as sore.

Yet he was obviously getting better. The little steps forward would temporarily get submerged by the powerful emotional swings, but they were definitely there. He could take deep breaths with less discomfort, roll out of bed, stand up, walk, sit and even concentrate for short periods. All he had to do was keep reminding himself of that.

This was clearly a time to be patient, grab what sleep he could and give his body a chance to recover. This happens only at the speed that nature allows, so it was no use willing the time away or insisting that his body got better more quickly.

Unfortunately, he couldn't simply be patient. Time still passed very slowly indeed.

By the third day in the HDU, his sense of merely being a body in the Process was reinforced when he had asked a nurse when his catheter and drainage tubes could come out, especially as the others had had theirs removed already. His notes had suggested that it would happen on the first or second day. All she could do was tell him that it would happen "soon". Then she went away.

That was no encouragement and the lack of an idea of when it would happen just served to drive down his morale. He was a man accustomed to working to a timetable. Not having any idea of when things were going to happen was draining his spirits.

Out of the blue that afternoon he got a visit from Annette, a kindly, dark haired nurse who said she had noticed during the ward rounds that he looked a bit fed up. She sat on his bed.

"How are you feeling?" she asked.

"In what way?" he said.

"How are you feeling inside. How is Ben coping?"

He drew a deep breath and burst into tears. It was such a shock.

She stood up and closed the curtains around his bed then sat down again and held his hand. He was weeping so much he couldn't speak. She sat like that for ten whole minutes while he unleashed his frustrations with his tears. The fear of the unknown, the isolation, the fatigue and the pain all built up to a blasted force that came pouring out of him without even a word being spoken.

An hour later she returned. She closed the curtains around him, asked him to lift his gown and then neatly eased his catheter out. It was an immensely practical move but it was once again a case of au revoir dignity. On the positive side, one less attachment made it a bit easier to move around.

The following day the drainage tubes and his neck cannula came out. Ben had asked another nurse when they could go. "Oh. Are they still in?" she said. After checking the state of the wound she simply got him to open his shirt and eased them out. As easy as that. No pain, no effort, no tugging. Just a small dressing to cover the holes for a short time.

Losing the connectors allowed him to be considerably more mobile. His joints were stiff and he was glad to start them moving again.

It was now possible to get out of bed in less than five minutes then shuffle off along the ward to get a bit of exercise or even – joy of joys – to visit the toilet. He did recognise that that was a rather strange notion.

From time to time, each member of the Cardiac Crew would troop off with hope in his eyes. Seven minutes later they would invariably return looking glum with that distinctive 'no luck yet' air about them. Morphine is known to cause severe blockages. Ben was suffering the same as the others. It was beginning to hurt. This was an issue he simply hadn't considered. Stealthily, its urgency and relevance started to build in his mind.

Early the next morning he needed an X-ray, which meant a trip to another part of the hospital. Exciting. Maybe he would see some natural daylight or even get a bit of sunshine.

Ethan rocked up with a wheelchair. "Benedict?" he said. "What's your date of birth, mate?"

Ben snarled. Honestly, this really isn't funny. It will be funny in years to come, but right now it's the pits and highly counterproductive. Then he gritted his teeth and said "Please call me Ben."

"Uh? Ok. That's cool. No problem. Hop in."

Ben really didn't want to be pushed around. His dignity insisted that he didn't want to be that helpless. It's never ever happened before and he really didn't want it to happen now.

"Could I walk?" said Ben.

"Sorry Benny-boy. No chance. It's a long way and you'd get too tired to make it. Hop in and I'll take you."

Benny-boy? Ben shuddered.

This was the first time he had ever sat in a wheelchair. He felt old and useless. It was a highly significant moment in his life and stirred up a thought that had been bothering him deeply. What had happened to the fiercely independent, unbreakable Ben? Where was the bravado and expectation that everything would turn out fine? Right at that moment it had abandoned him.

He sat, unhappy that he needed a cock-sure kid to transport him.

Off they sailed through the ward, into a lift and along another corridor. Ethan reversed through one of the heavy doors then saw his colleague Denzel. His attention was diverted and they started chatting while they walked, dragging Ben backwards along the corridor in his open-backed gown.

He was miserable. How many more indignities would he have to go through? Where was the basic respect? Had he really become this incapable and invisible?

This was also, of course, confirmation of what had been worrying him – his kids' dad wasn't actually invincible. They had often seen him with minor knocks but he always bounced back. There was nothing he

71

couldn't do. Or so he thought they thought. Now here was indisputable evidence that he was broken and couldn't even command enough respect to be pushed down a corridor forwards.

That hurt a whole lot more than the sore chest and back or even the indignities of being asked about his bowel movements, lifting his gown to have a catheter removed or breaking down in tears in front of a complete stranger, even if she was encouraging it.

Chapter 10 – The Roller Coaster

"Life is a roller coaster. It has its ups and downs, its thrills, its terrors. Once in a while it just randomly breaks down."

The X-ray presumably confirmed that his heart was on track because the following morning he got some good news at last.

There was a bed available for him on Christopher Ward and he could be moved within an hour or so.

This time he was pleased to see Ethan and forgave him his earlier failings. As he was wheeled out of the HDU he felt his spirits lifting. This was another little step forward. In a day or two he could be on his way home.

The Cardiac Crew was on the move. Clark and Kelvin had moved on the previous day although poor old Veda stayed behind for more observations and tests.

When Ben got to Christopher Ward it was clean, calm and full of sunlight. He was wheeled to a bed beside a huge window overlooking a copse of trees opposite. That made him feel a lot better. Fantastic. He hadn't seen 'outside' for what seemed like an age.

The new ward sister was Alica. She welcomed him in and said "What would you like to be called?"

He could have kissed her. "Ben, please."

"Certainly, Ben. If you have any questions please ask. Our part is to keep you comfortable until you are well enough to go home. We'll take bloods every morning and you'll have your pills twice a day. We'd also like you to get up as much as you can. Get dressed if possible and walk as far as you can each day. There are plenty of chairs along the corridors so you can rest if you need to."

What a difference.

In short order his dressings were taken off and he was told he could have a shower when he wanted to, although he should try to protect the wound a bit so water couldn't get in through the stitches.

Now that he was more mobile he tried to do more things for himself. Alica noticed him lean over to pick up his bag of books. She was pleasant about it, but Ben knew he had received a right royal dressing down.

He was NOT to lift anything of weight, even a small bag with a couple of books in. To help the chest heal properly he shouldn't lift anything above one kilogram for six weeks after the operation.

It sounded like a ridiculously small weight, yet Ben was convinced by the fire in her eyes that she wasn't exaggerating. She was really firm about it. He had read that in other parts of the world they used two or even three kilos as a guide, yet she convinced him to work with the lower limit. He was reminded of Charlie's words: "You only have one shot at this."

The rules were simple. If it was too heavy, wait for someone to help you. Even taking hold of a tray of food would be too much. Let the server place it down for you; do not try to take it off them.

Ben really struggled with this ruling at first. Basically he wouldn't be able to contribute to running the house when he got out of here. No ironing, no tidying, no clearing up for him for a while. It seemed unnatural. Running the house had always been a shared activity with Jamie. Yet he would have to learn the patience not to do it.

Shortly afterwards, the day picked up again with the arrival of his evening meal. It was delicious and served with a lovely smile by a young lady who introduced herself as Karen. She seemed to revel in the job.

Another huge difference. It was almost enough to make you feel better.

"Would you like some food? Erm, Ben?" she had asked after reading his nameplate. And there was choice. After the limitations of the last few days, this was as good as a white glove service. It made him feel wonderful. Human.

Relevant. Even verging on significant. If this carried on he may even get to feel cared about.

'Wonderful' lasted about three hours into the evening, when he experienced Lin Woo for the first time. She was a physically small and cheerful nurse who made everyone smile. Someone they could hear crashing around well before she arrived in a room.

"Benedict? What your date of birth?" she yelled, then, without a pause "Have your bowels moved yet? No? I get you laxative."

He felt like screaming. "Please. Please. It's Ben. And no they haven't. Please, call me Ben."

Another false dawn. Maybe Alica was too good to be true. So far about half of all the clinicians who had spoken to him had ignored his name written on the board above his bed. Yet they had all surely read it. It was infuriating, although he wasn't sure if he should be more annoyed at his own impatience or his perceived lack of consideration or respect.

"Don't sweat the small stuff," he would tell himself and then promptly ignored his own advice.

The Cardiac Crew were all in wards off the same corridor with the exception of Veda, whose complications had extended to questions about whether he needed a pacemaker to be inserted or not, so was still in HDU.

Sometimes his heart fluttered like a butterfly and the beat was so erratic that the pacemaker appeared to be inevitable. The next few hours it would function perfectly well and seemed to have righted itself. In the end they decided to install one and monitor it over a period of months. If it turned out to be needed, they would leave it in; if not, they could easily turn it off in one of his follow-up sessions.

Ben was pleased to see that Bert was in his ward. He liked his company.

He seemed so solid and reliable, like a piece of teak. He sat quietly, simply riding the wave of disappointment of having no visitors. His wife couldn't get there and his son would only visit if he couldn't possibly avoid it. Bert was lonely yet reluctant to admit it and withdrew into himself for hours at a time, patiently allowing time to pass while he put up with it all. Despite that, he and Ben enjoyed quiet and private discussions in the corner of the ward. He was such a nice, gentle man that Ben couldn't fail to enjoy his presence.

He was clearly very uncomfortable from being bunged up. He hadn't been to the toilet for six days and it was hurting a lot. Nor had Ben, who spent more than enough time and effort heaving and straining with no luck, wary of straining too hard just in case. It would have made a hell of a reason for having to open him up again.

Lin Woo was good to her word and added some powerful laxatives to their twice daily diet of drugs.

At five a.m. on his second day on Christopher Ward, she clattered in and started her rounds with Ben.

"Benedict? What your date of birth? I need to take some blood."

"Ben. My name is Ben. Please call me Ben."

"OK. No problem. Ben. Now let's try and find that vein. I'm as blind as a bat at this time of day," she said as she dug away at his arm.

Twelve hours later she was back.

"Benedict? What your date of birth? Have your bowels moved yet?"

"Ben. Please. Ben. Please, please, please."

"Ben. Yes."

Then at five the following morning she was back after he had had a sleepless night shifting around desperately trying to find a comfortable position to allow his back to relax. "Benedict? What your date of birth? Have your bowels moved tonight?"

"Ben. Ben. Ben. My name is Ben. PLEASE CALL ME BEN" he growled. He was tired, in pain and his innards were in agony from the morphine-induced blockage. He was completely and utterly fed up with this simple request being ignored as it vigorously reinforced his feeling of being an irrelevant body rather than a person.

"Of course I will, Ben. Don't I always? Now, have your bowels moved yet?"

He wasn't alone, though. Everyone got it. Bert was called Albert, Jon was Jonathan, Mike was Michael. All were irritated by it to a greater or lesser extent. It wasn't a complaint about Lin Woo, because she was so naturally cheerful that people couldn't help but smile, as long as she wasn't treating them.

No, hers was just one more part of the impersonal Process that made them feel so irrelevant as people whilst at the same time receiving truly world class medical care. The Cardiac Crew all felt slightly guilty because they acknowledged that if they worked in a situation where there was an unrelenting demand from a constant turnover of bodies then they would almost certainly fall into being impersonal, too.

It would only be natural.

Poor old Snowy got it the worst. He had been called Snowy since the week after he was born, yet his birth certificate read Christopher. So Christopher he was, to Lin Woo. He was also 84 years old, very confused and deaf as a doorpost. Lin Woo's way of getting through was to shout his name louder and louder. That wasn't funny at two in the morning, although the others in different wards thought so.

On the third day on the ward there came a sea-change. As usual Bert shuffled towards the toilet more in hope than expectation. Ten minutes later he came out of the toilet with the broadest grin on his face and twinkle in his eye. "That," he said to Ben in his most rural accent, "was the second best experience of my life after my wedding night with my Elsie."

Ben laughed. And it didn't hurt because he was genuinely delighted for Bert. Two hours later he had a similar grin on his face. What an incredible relief.

Visiting times were always looked forward to, although not a lot was said. Each day Jamie travelled in to the hospital, shared the space and updates with him for a couple of hours then drove home again to deal with the calls and keep the rest of the family informed. It was almost a full time activity in itself. It was exhausting.

She grew to despise the journey. What was previously a route leading to the buzz and variety of an exciting city became a track she felt compelled to travel to sit and watch her husband struggle through a trial that she knew full well could easily turn the wrong way. The worry and niggling doubt about the future was ensuring that her sleep was limited and the constant need to keep people updated meant that she always seemed to be behind with her own work on a daily basis.

Ben was eager for her to spend time on herself and get to a position where she felt she had caught up. He wasn't exactly going anywhere and it would only be for a couple of days. She was having none of that. Even if he didn't appreciate it, she knew that just being there was giving him emotional support and strength. It meant that someone was on his side.

Sometimes their daughter Nia was able to join Jamie. Ben didn't realise until much later how much she had been drawn into the whole situation. Initially she had been annoyed by his determination to think positively about the operation because she wanted him to at least acknowledge that it was possible for things to go wrong.

Once he was in hospital the visits were tough. Dad was indestructible, wasn't he? She couldn't even remember him crying before. Yet here he was in hospital, vulnerable and weepy. Like a sponge being wrung out. No wonder her brothers were so reluctant to visit. When he had looked across the HDU ward at Clark and Veda's families visiting, it began to dawn on Ben how hard it was for their families. He simply didn't make the connection to his own situation.

After visiting, Nia would then have to go home and work to keep Jamie's mind occupied on things other than the hospital visits. It was very hard to take.

The evening after he was moved to Christopher Ward, Nia brought in a roller massager and used it to roll his back with a wonderfully firm massage. It was almost miraculous how much relief that gave so quickly.

It had been a good day. The increasingly painful blockage had been cleared and Nia had found a way that just may be able to resolve that constant pain between his shoulder blades.

The roller coaster had changed direction again.

Chapter 11 – Blood Runs Thin

"The final hurdle is no higher than the rest but feels like it is." Jeremy Chin

Almost as soon as he had arrived on Christopher Ward, Ben had been asking when he could go home.

"It depends."

"On what?"

"Some of your numbers in your bloods aren't quite right yet."

"Which numbers?"

"INR."

"What's INR? Is that a good thing or a bad thing? Am I too high or too low or what?" He'd never heard of it.

INR stands for the International Normalized Ratio, which is a laboratory measure of how long it takes blood to clot. Normal blood usually takes ten to fourteen seconds to do so and that translates to an INR figure of about 1.1. After a heart operation, though, you need thinner blood as there are risks with some potentially very unpleasant consequences.

Because of his atrial flutter Ben was a slightly higher risk, so his INR count was important.

A low INR means that blood can clot too easily and so there is a chance of a clump breaking off and in too many cases causing a stroke. Too high an INR means that it doesn't clot quickly enough so there is the ever present risk of bleeding continuously from simple knocks and, in the more extreme cases, bleeding out.

You really need an INR of between 2.0 and 3.0 to significantly reduce the risks. Talk to a specialist about numbers outside that range and they quail as the risks increase enormously.

If anything, a slightly higher INR is marginally preferable to a lower one although neither would be a choice. Yes, it's that serious. Sensibly, Ben thought "OK. I need to know about this."

In fact it meant that he would have to take an anticoagulant such as Warfarin until it had stabilised. That would have impacts on his life outside hospital, not least that he would need to avoid certain foods and be careful about what he drank while he was taking it. Cranberries suddenly became his most longed-for taste when he was told that they were completely off the menu. No juice, no sauce. Torment.

Yet he wasn't being informed about things like that. All he was being told was that he couldn't go home.

Each morning he would be woken up, endure the challenges of Lin Woo and wait in hope for the results. Today could be the day. It gave him solace in the early hours when sleep wouldn't come or when he was disturbed by the pain or a disturbance somewhere else on the ward.

Then it would shatter and infuriate him when the only message he received was "No, you won't be going home today" without a reason. He begged to be told the results and not just given the considered conclusion.

He was desperate to leave. He still couldn't sleep and he had conclusively proven that hospital really isn't a place to try to rest or to get better. If he was at home he would have slightly more chance.

Each day he felt his hope rise and then get crushed. It seemed as if the only good thing was that he could give Lin Woo a positive answer about his bowels. His morale was taking a real hiding even though he was doing everything he possibly could to get ready to leave.

He was standing, stretching, walking and even practising climbing up and down stairs. He trained himself to get smoothly out of bed, which was no mean feat when he wasn't supposed to use his arms to push or pull. He developed techniques to carry small items through the heavy doors in the corridors. He was doing what he could. All he needed was the thumbs up to go.

On his walks along the corridors, he was increasing his distance each time. That felt good. He even tried to keep up with Kelvin but he was like a man possessed. He had been given his life back and marched up and down the wards like a stallion for most of each day, building up his strength and stamina.

Meanwhile Clark had already been sent home and was texting to keep everyone amused and up to date with his progress. He was already sleeping through the night and was elated with the extra life he felt he had been given. Mind you, even a small effort would leave him shattered the following day with very little energy.

He picked up on Ben's frustrations. "Pls don't let it get to you. They're only doing their jobs and between me and you mate they have done a fantastic job on me. It will be sorted so keep your chin up." Timing is all. That worked a treat. Two minutes later came another. "On a good note, mate, I'm living life to the full and just ordered myself two brand new urine bottles on eBay." Ben laughed out loud. How to keep things in perspective.

Ben was sent for another echocardiogram, this one presumably to check on progress. Ethan's chum Denzel whizzed him along to the echo room and left him sitting alone in the wheelchair in a cold corridor. He sat there and fumed impotently.

He wasn't told anything about the results. Actually he found out later that that was for reasons of medical best practice, but that wasn't the point. Right now his three-year-old persona was in charge. He was supposed to be an adult taking responsibility for his own health yet important results were being kept away from him. Was he so emotionally brittle that 'they' thought he couldn't handle it? Or maybe 'they' thought he wasn't intelligent enough to understand?

The lack of information provided was getting to him once again.

As there were no alarmed looks he guessed that he was supposed to presume that no news was good news and that his recovery was roughly on track.

He could physically feel his attitude turning sour and he didn't like that. By the time he was dumped back into the ward, it positively stank.

At least there was Karen, cheerfully offering him an afternoon cup of tea or coffee. And a biscuit if he fancied one. He felt his mood lift. A smile is such a tiny gesture and costs nothing at all, yet so often it can transform someone's day. It certainly did it for Ben.

An hour later another text arrived from the prolific Clark asking how he was. Ben grumbled back.

Quick as a flash came Clark's response. "Go for a sh#t and rest your brains, mate. It's just a blip. Trust me."

Once again, he laughed out loud. First a smile from Karen and now an unexpected belly laugh courtesy of Clark to remind him about the good things in life. That was better. It was bizarre how quickly his mood would swing from high to low and back again. It wasn't that quick in real life, was it?

On her visit that afternoon, Jamie handed him a small parcel. He opened it and saw it was a present from their son's girlfriend's mother, whom they had only ever briefly met once.

He turned towards the windows and tears rolled silently down his cheeks.

It was a generous gesture, that's for sure, and he was delighted with the surprise out of the blue. Yet did it justify tears again? No, the tears were tears of fatigue, pain and regularly squashed hope. He was surrounded by humanity yet he felt alone. It seemed as if every time something moved forward, another half dozen things would pop up to impede him again.

He really did need to get out of here and get some sleep otherwise he'd end up a wreck, justifying being here in the first case.

He begged Alica to be allowed to leave or at least to let him know the results and what they meant. She couldn't let him leave, but the following day, contrary to the rules, she quietly told him the result – it was 1.6 – before he was told the conclusion. The news wasn't good, but at least he was being treated as if he were a part of it, which made it more palatable. That small gesture made a massive difference to his day. The disappointment was now just a small hiccup in the grand scheme of things and not a crushing blow to his soul.

He even offered his poop grade as a three or a four on most days. At least that was stable.

So was the relentless humour from Clark. "Had a relaxing one all day" he texted, "or as I call it being a totally lazy b#stard. The walk I did on Tuesday burnt me out and it will take some time to reboot. I keep telling myself I'm fixed but my body tells me I'm jumping before I can walk."

Then "Guess who woke up at 8.30 today? I'm a party animal." Ben always felt buoyed up when a text arrived. They were always direct and to the point. They also gave him a hint of what to expect in his own first few days out of hospital. "Pain free today but still short of breath."

Good news from Veda. His pacemaker had finally been installed so he was on track to be discharged. He was now on the main wards with everyone else.

"May I leave?" Ben asked Astella, the nurse who had been involved in all of the INR conversations.

"Unfortunately not yet. Your INR isn't right and your heart rate is still fluctuating a bit more than we want. We need to see better results before you can go. For all other things you are fine. It's just these numbers we want to see improve first."

On the tenth day of what was now feeling like his incarceration, a new consultant came to do the rounds.

"What are you doing in here? You're too well."

"I know. That's what I've been telling everyone."

"Well you can leave. On condition that you get seen by the surgeon within a fortnight, your INR is tracked and there is someone with you all the time for the first ten days or so. We'll make sure your GP knows exactly what to do too. Go and get your stuff ready."

Ben was elated. Another one to kiss. His spirits soared even faster than they had plummeted this morning when told that his INR was still too low.

All of a sudden he had something he could do that was within his control. He started with a call to Jamie to request a lift home, "and please remember to bring a cushion", then followed it with a bouncy stride down the corridor to say farewell and collect the Cardiac Crew's contact details.

He had to remember to open the doors with his back so the grin on his face could fit through. Turned out that

Kelvin had been told he could go home on that day too. Clark had already gone. It was evidently a clear-out before the weekend.

He asked Alica to pass on his thanks to all the nurses, Isaac and Denzel the wheelchair men, Karen the white glove waiter and to Massimo and his team. "And Annette. Please thank Annette. She really helped me when I was in a really bad place. And anyone else who knows me." He felt like he was giving a speech at the Oscars, so heady was his excitement.

"Oh, and you have been wonderful, Alica. Thank you so much. You made me feel relevant and that has been invaluable to me. Would you kiss that consultant for me please? Don't fancy it myself."

Next it was a visit to the pharmacist to collect a stash of tablets. He had four different pills to take each day plus an aspirin. He set a little goal to be off those four as soon as he possibly could.

He carefully packed up his belongings – one item at a time – and waited for his lift to arrive.

When Jamie and Nia walked in through the door with his coat he was almost delirious with excitement. They were the most beautiful vision in the world.

"Let's go!"

Then it was down the stairs and past the smokers at the front door. "Why?" he muttered as he did every time he saw them assembled there. He pushed them out of his mind. Not his problem right now. He had the rest of his own life to get on with.

The fresh air made his head spin.

It took them five minutes to get him into the car. He let Nia open the car door for him and he backed onto the seat before carefully swivelling round to face the front. He had to be careful not to use his hands and put any accidental strain on his chest.

That was considerably more difficult than it seemed because it went against every instinct he had developed since first getting into a car. Once he was in, he slid the cushion in between his chest and the seatbelt.

Jamie started the car and pulled away.

She was terrified.

He was elated.

His frustrations, anger and feeling of helplessness earlier that morning had been replaced by a nervous excitement. What's next?

As they drove out of the hospital grounds he felt a wave of relief. He hadn't enjoyed the last ten days - was it seriously only ten? - although he had learned a lot. Especially about himself.

He felt free.

He had been in for three more days than he had expected and that had been more than enough. How other patients manage to stay sane during long stays in hospital was beyond his imagination at that time. But right now he was getting out.

Another little step that felt like a mighty stride.

Now his recovery could start in earnest, beginning with a nice rest in his own bed.

Chapter 12 – Home Sweet Home

*"I am not the same having seen the moon shine
on the other side of the world."*
Mary Anne Radmacher

It had only been ten days. Two or three more than he had expected, so in the grand scheme of things that wasn't a problem. It was just everything else.

He felt excited to be free. He could start the recovery process. And yet… He had gone into hospital feeling confident and strong. Now he was feeling fragile and more vulnerable than at any time he could remember.

It was a nerve wracking journey.

The car seemed to seek out every bump and pothole in the road that jarred through his body and headed straight for his chest. Jamie drove as carefully as Ben had done when he had driven each of their newly-born children home.

In the silence of the journey, he took a mental inventory of his situation.

He was stressed. Big time. Most of it self-inflicted as well, because he hadn't let go.

He hadn't slept much in the last ten days and was tired and irritable.

He hadn't been able to trust his own fortitude for a mere ten days – even while he was getting better.

He had broken down crying at least three times and he was put out by even the smallest things.

He had expected to be nursed and looked after while he was in hospital and instead felt like he had been churned through a Process, there for only as long as absolutely essential and then shoved out as soon as possible. A hugely impersonal Process that had been applied to the most personal moments of his life up to that point. Talk about a mismatch of expectations.

He was no longer invincible dad. Things would be different from now on. It was unavoidable.

He couldn't even make a pot of tea because a kettle of water was too heavy for him to lift.

Jamie clearly wasn't sleeping either and was visibly exhausted. He desperately wanted her to concentrate on her own world and leave him to get on with recovering. Yet he couldn't do that because he was still dependent on having someone around to either do or help him do so many things. "That," she said much later, "was the scariest time of my life apart from my mother dying."

In that instant he felt low. All of the personal traits he had honestly believed he could depend upon had been found wanting under pressure. Meanwhile it felt like the car was bouncing violently around what felt like a mogul ski run topped with corrugated iron.

He shook himself. This way of thinking would only ever lead to one thing. Stop it. Surely there are some bright points? Well, yes there were, he decided.

He felt battered and bruised, and that was OK. In fact, it was good, because he knew that it was only temporary and he could actually do something to help to sort it.

He had already found that climbing stairs, walking up the smallest slope or even standing up from a chair could be challenging; inhaling fresh air was intoxicating and made his head spin. Yet he knew for certain that these would improve rapidly with a bit of time and application. The first time you do something is always the hardest. Everything gets easier with repetition.

He was not alone. He had forged an enormously close bond with a terrific group of people in a very short time period. And his family had been incredibly supportive. Jamie was making herself ill trying to look after him.

And his background setup was tidy. His papers were all in order AND there was some magnificent televised sport coming up over the next few weeks

There was something to build on. Go on, Ben, pick yourself up. Turn that frown upside down. Count your blessings and accept that all that's happened is but a small setback. So some of your expectations didn't come in? Well that's the way life is. Now stop feeling sorry for yourself and get on with it.

He concluded that all in all it wasn't bad. The defect had been repaired and all he had to do was get himself back into shape.

Mind you, he was already mildly missing the hubbub and busy-ness of the hospital and the presence of his new besties.

A few days earlier, Clark had travelled home by train. He was too big and solid to go in the small car his wife had available, so it was more practical to travel by rail to as close to home as possible. The railway staff had been fantastic in looking after him in his wheelchair. Once there, he had been collected in a big SUV.

On the same day as Ben left, Kelvin was collected and headed home, determined to start laying tiles that very afternoon. He had a life to lead and couldn't wait to get on with it.

Poor old Veda stayed in for another three days until the pacemaker issue was finally resolved.

The Cardiac Crew were stepping into a new phase in their lives. It would be fascinating to see how they all handled the next few weeks. They hoped they would hear from Bert, who was also due to be collected that afternoon by his reluctant son and taken home to be looked after by his beloved Elsie.

Arriving back home Ben looked around.

Everything was the same; yet everything was different. His world had been forever changed in such a short period of time

His brain felt tired, dull witted and slow. And he temporarily felt like a burden because he had been released only on condition that there was someone with him all the time for the first ten days or so. He simply had to make himself learn to live with it.

He had been disappointed in himself for allowing his attitude to turn sour that time in the wheelchair. Now he needed to make up for that and showing a bit of patience would be a start. It was for his own good, after all.

After greeting the house, the first thing he wanted was to go for a walk. He felt so pleased with his release that he wanted to get on with it as soon as he could. He had already mentally earmarked a few target distances.

They lived on the side of a hill, which meant that whenever he left the house it was immediately either uphill or downhill. Not level. He managed just twenty slow metres up the hill with Nia before having to sit on a wall to rest. Then they turned around and went back home. It had taken about fifteen minutes.

Yet what joy he felt. He had completed a forty metre trek in fresh air. He was exhausted and elated.

Now, though, he had an inkling of how big a task he faced to get back. There was no choice but to start slowly because he simply wasn't capable to doing anything other than that. He wondered whether Kelvin really was doing his tiling. He hoped not.

He remembered what Charlie had said to him: to start slowly and build up. Step by step. It will take twelve weeks. Don't push it too hard or too early. Consistency and determination would be key. You only have the one chance for your breastbone to heal.

In the early evening he managed a second walk, to a pole about two hundred metres from home. It took him an age, yet that was the first of his targets and it felt good to achieve it so soon.

He was walking just as the hospital had instructed, except now he was in the fresh air and encountering inclines. It felt challenging but good.

He went to bed early that evening, looking forward to a comfortable and undisturbed sleep. Alas, he quickly discovered that he couldn't lie down flat because his chest, back and neck all hurt, it was difficult to breathe and adjusting position was a real challenge. The hospital beds all had electronically-adjustable backs. No such luxuries at home. So he carefully rolled out and moved downstairs to see if he could find a way to rest on their reclining chair.

Jamie and Nia had also set up a V-shaped stack of cushions on the settee. This would be better as it was just about high enough for him to be able to roll off and get his feet on the floor without having to push or pull much.

In those first days, the roller massager was in almost constant use. Nia would grind it in to his muscles and ease some of the stiffness.

It hurt like hell.

It was heavenly.

Then there was the question of what to do about the compression socks. The advice he had been given during his pre-op meeting was to wear them during the day for up to six weeks although that meant taking them off each evening and putting them back on in the morning. Easier said than done as Jamie and Nia pushed, heaved and swore to get them beyond his heel and up his calf.

None of that mattered just yet. He was home.

It was one more small and highly significant step.

Chapter 13 – Steady As You Go

"Change. But start slowly. For direction is more important than speed."   *Paulo Coelho*

On the second day home he walked four hundred metres before turning round. That felt good.

It would need to be gradual. Incremental. In time he would feel ready to begin some of these projects he had planned. Not yet though. He was still fuzzy headed and his concentration was limited. He was shocked at how quickly any strength he had built up in the months before the operation had disappeared. It would be extremely easy to sit back and do nothing and it took determination to get up and move.

Years ago, when he had stopped playing competitive sport, he had gradually allowed himself to stop moving. It crept up on him one day at a time. And once you stop, it gets harder both physically and mentally to get moving again. Naturally, he had stiffened up, which made it even more of a challenge to move. So he hadn't, preferring to take the easy path. Soon his body had become so stiff that it became painful to move at all. So he moved even less. Next thing he knew, he was in almost permanent pain. It had taken him an enormous amount of effort and application to start moving again and slowly get rid of the pain. "Motion is lotion" became another adage he carried through life.

He would not and could not allow himself to stop now and let that happen again, although he knew it would be hard. The way his back felt was enough to remind him, so each day he made himself walk just a little bit further than the previous day, revelling in the company and encouragement of Jamie or Nia.

In their own first weeks at home, both Clark and Veda reported that they got cold and out of breath, even though the weather was warm. Clark was also getting pain in his back and discomfort on both sides of his chest. "I just think we need to carry on as normal but take our time doing it, mate," he texted. Then another one saying that he was "Getting some grief with the healing process taking its time. Stick with it, mate." It was further proof to Ben that simply sharing how you feel about an experience can be enormously encouraging.

Kelvin later told them that he had indeed managed to lay a few small tiles within two days of getting home, so he was quite pleased with himself. Ben shuddered a little at the prospect. Charlie's warnings were vivid.

Ben made sure he varied the routes he walked and played counting games with himself to try to sharpen his brain. That was tiring. In the first week he was definitely dull of mind and found he would soon drop off for a nap after getting back. As Clark and Veda were confirming, it was a slow process. Yet each minor success gave him a little bit more confidence.

Each day he felt a little bit stronger and more flexible than the day before and in turn that made it easier to get up and go. Not that he needed special motivation. The sun was out, he was out and he had a plan for recovery.

Within a week he hit his major target of ten thousand steps in a day for the first time and celebrated by walking very slowly up the hill to the park where he could sit and look at the beauty and activity of his hometown below him.

As he looked out there came another pair of perfectly timed texts from Clark. "Now I've got piles," and, causing Ben yet again to laugh out loud, he wrote "My walking is getting better and not so breathless either. But I walk like I'm mincing."

Ben was still unable to lie flat though, and each night was fractured. He slept a maximum of three hours at a time although even that was a big improvement on when he first got back. That he had had a reclining chair and a massager had been strokes of luck rather than being down to forward planning, and they were put into almost permanent use to provide him some comfort.

Friends then loaned him a small camping kettle that held enough water for two cups. That meant it was light enough for him to safely fill and lift. He could make his own coffee and tea. He could also make a coffee or tea for Jamie. That was important to him. It was a tiny bit of independence.

Every little step helped.

Part of the terms of his discharge was to visit his own GP and organise checks for his INR. He was given no doubt that he was to be left to his own devices except for having his INR checked regularly. He was slightly taken aback because he had expected his progress to be tracked and monitored as a matter of course. Yet if that's the way it had to be, then he should accept and get on with it.

He did insist that the 'regular' INR check should be weekly as he had been reminded of the potential consequences of an out of range count and wanted to keep a close eye on it.

He was given no particular advice other than to "start slowly and take it easy; don't rush things," and come back in six weeks. The INR information was more detailed and included dietary advice on a website that listed the foods he should avoid while taking the anti-coagulants. He presumed that meant his existing consumption was considered to be OK.

In time he would realise that, of all the things he could have done to accelerate his recovery, this was the biggest miss. All he had needed was to be told to drink two litres of water a day then see if he could start to replace processed foods or those with extra salt or sugar with natural foods. Without imposing it as a strict diet, that would have worked for him and his natural inquisitiveness would have caused him to try different combinations and tastes.

As he got stronger in the second week at home, the need to be accompanied eased and Jamie and Nia felt they could trust him to take it steady.

He ranged further and further afield, walking at a steady pace for longer and longer.

He started to love it. He was putting no strain or threat on his chest and was happy to be in control of how much activity he did.

Late that week, just twenty one days after the operation, a family member asked him "Do you feel better yet? After all, the operation is over and done with and you're fine now, aren't you?"

The answer was "No, although I'm better today than yesterday and better yesterday than the day before, so it will come."

He was tempted to ask whether they had any idea of what the operation had entailed but stopped himself. They didn't know; why would they? It was going to be a slow process and he would have to get used to questions like that.

Meanwhile Clark was reporting progress. He was still sleeping soundly, walking a small amount each day and felt "like a teenager with a new lease of life." He had worked out that taking a painkiller at four in the morning meant that he would sleep well, was in control of the pain and, although the scar on his chest was tight, it was healing. He was even starting to take some really deep breaths. But he was getting bored so was thinking of going back to work already.

That week he had had a savage coughing fit whilst alone. "I thought I was going to die and cuddled my towel for about an hour. So go steady if it happens to you." Where was Ben's sympathy? His immediate thought in that exchange was that Superman used a Linus blanket, which wasn't exactly sympathetic. In truth, Ben had been lucky and had only coughed on a few occasions. When he did, though, they really ripped through him. A coughing fit must have been terrifying.

Ben said that he was tempted to write a short book about their experiences. Clark had texted back "You could name it the ups and downs of a heart attack by three stud strippers." The comment was so off the wall that Ben yet again laughed out loud at a text.

Mid-way through week three, Jamie commented "You don't look very happy."

"That's because I'm having to concentrate on absolutely everything I do for every second of every minute of every day."

The wariness against taking a knock or falling over made him give 100% focus to everything he did. His INR was still up and down and he was hypersensitive to any potential danger. He was enjoying himself, although the concentration left him with little room for multi-tasking. It was like asking him to walk and chew gum at the same time. Not that he chewed gum, of course, as that was another of his grumpy old man hates.

Concentrating was very tiring.

Chapter 14 – Small Steps

"The man who moves a mountain begins by carrying away small stones." Confucius

At the end of the third week after the operation, ten days at home, he slept for nine hours in a single night. Admittedly it was in three chunks, but it was a highly significant marker.

By now the constant massage of his back, walking and gentle stretching was starting to have an effect, his chest wound was beginning to heal and he could take a shower without having to protect it. It was hugely encouraging. It also helped that the weather was fabulous. Sunshine on his shoulder would always make Ben happy and cause him to mentally sing John Denver's classic song.

He had not needed to take painkillers regularly since the second day at home, so he stopped taking them.

One of the four tablets down. Three to go.

Another step.

That weekend he, Jamie and Nia all agreed he could stop wearing the compression socks. The decision took a whole load of daily effort and frustration out of their lives with one fell swoop.

Another drop of freedom. Another small step.

Veda and Clark also abandoned their stockings at roughly the same time. Veda was delighted that he could now let the sun get to his legs. Clark joked that he had been "Losing street cred with the kids."

Apparently "The man scar doesn't work when you have your wife's stockings on," even though he had painted a seam on the back "with some gravy granules and a sharpie pen."

Ben enjoyed inventing little games to enliven the humdrum of daily life and by now they were referring to 'weeks ATO', or weeks After The Operation. He was already at the end of week three, which meant that there should only be another three to go before he could think about doing a lot more, assuming Charlie was accurate.

He could barely wait.

So far not one of his eagerly anticipated small projects had even been looked at.

He was still dull of mind and preferred the sensation of getting a bit stronger each day over sitting down and getting organised. Nevertheless, he had been firm with himself over any temptation to watch daytime TV. He only watched if there was a good sporting event available. Instead, he had tried to stimulate his brain with Sudoku, world news and walking in nature.

He was pleasantly surprised at his own self-control. He had expected to be disheartened by the need to start slowly and not to take any risks whatsoever. Instead he was thriving on it.

He did need something to do with his hands, though. He had planned on teaching himself to knit, yet that didn't hold any appeal for him just now. There was, however, a large pile of Lego blocks in the loft taking up space that had been a little itch in the back of his mind for years.

So instead of learning new software packages, practising other languages, reading his backlog of mind-enhancing books or learning to knit, he sorted Lego bricks, built models, watched sport on TV and completed Sudoku puzzles. With the Lego he was actively creating something and there was no requirement for deep or meaningful concentration.

It was exactly what he needed at this stage of his ongoing recovery.

In theory it is feasible to drive four weeks after the operation. In practice Ben was too nervous of the damage that any crash may cause so he didn't. Much as he hated to admit it, his ability to concentrate and focus fully still wasn't up to scratch either. He had also seen a fantastic poster from a roadside in New Zealand that read "Other people make mistakes" and that stuck with him. If there was going to be a bump, he might not be the cause.

He had already risked a train journey and had felt very nervous being surrounded by crowds of people with sharp elbows and not being in a position to control the speed they travelled at.

A few days before that trip he had started to notice a strange popping and grinding sound coming from his chest. He hoped it was the sign of healing, rather than any damage. It did make him more cautious, though. He would wait until he got proper clearance from the cardiac team, which was supposed to take place six weeks after the operation.

He was regularly walking over ten thousand steps a day, including a daily climb up the hill from town. He had already managed to do it non-stop, although that took a long time.

He was even getting slightly faster and had set a longer term goal to take on the precipitous set of two hundred steps known as Jacob's Ladder.

It is always encouraging to achieve small targets, especially when they represent a challenge. Another work mantra.

By the middle of week four ATO Ben's scar was settling down, but there were still small scabs on the holes where the draining tubes had been. The surgeon had done a very neat job of sewing him up so it was unlikely to be too prominent or obvious in time. The large bobble at the top had shrunk away, to his delight. One day he may even be able to take his shirt off in public, although he didn't feel that was an option just yet.

Clark was pleased with his, too. "Chicks love a good scar, apparently," he texted. Then he added that "They used a chainsaw to get through my manly body," to add praise to the sewing skills of the surgeon. It was uncanny. These texts all seemed to land at exactly the right time. Ben found it useful to compare their relative rates of improvement. They were all different, of course, yet there were so many parallels also many similarities. That made a big difference. He was not alone.

By the end of the week four Ben started to sleep in his own bed. That was fantastic. Admittedly he was on his back and could only manage short bursts of a few hours at a time, but he was in a bed.

Another step forward.

It wasn't all good news though. As his exercise was limited to walking, he was noticing a lot of muscle loss.

He would need to add rebuilding muscles to his own meaning of recovery.

He had grudgingly acknowledged that recovery by his own definition was likely to take more than six weeks. He set an interim target of being back to work part time after eight or nine weeks although inwardly he hoped to do it sooner. A lot would depend on what the surgeon said to him in his six week review.

He ate pretty well. His diet was good. Or so he thought, anyway. He hadn't really changed much because he felt he hadn't needed to and he hadn't been told he should. As a result he hadn't lost any weight. He didn't really care about that though. It wasn't an issue. It was only relevant because he had set it as one of his nice-to-have targets for this post-operation period.

Emotionally, he was still experiencing big swings. He had read that it is common for people to suffer a major down or even depression after a big operation. While he was determined not to allow his emotions to dominate his spirit, sometimes it was unavoidable.

Jamie was concerned about his health. He still had an atrial flutter and his breathing was often erratic when he was asleep. She couldn't help but be aware of this and was permanently on edge waiting for him to breathe again after a gap. It made it impossible for her to drop into any deep sleep so she was exhausted and feeling as groggy as he was.

Fatigue meant that he got snappy, she got snappy; he tried to withdraw and she followed him; she wanted to talk, he didn't. Basically, he wanted to be left alone to recover and that wasn't happening.

Yet he was also lonely, despite the text contacts with Clark and Veda. There was nobody he could talk with face to face who could empathise.

People would call or visit to say hello, after which the conversation quickly dried up. He had had the operation so all was fixed, wasn't it? Sure, he had a few stitches to get over and the scar would be a dramatic reminder of it all, but surely he was nearly better now?

He would tell them that a deep cut takes six to eight weeks to recover and even a soft tissue injury can take eight, so no, not yet. Just because you can't see the stitches doesn't mean that the injury is fully healed. They would murmur assent yet he felt they were thinking that he should be better by now. And he sometimes felt like a fraud because on the surface he looked fine.

Week five saw a plateau in his progress and in those low times he got very circumspect. He thought about his life, his family, his marriage, his kids and his 'career' of permanently making himself redundant.

Is this it? Is it worth all this effort?

Week six came. It was as if a switch had been thrown. Charlie had been absolutely right. Almost to the day.

He had slept through the night for the first time, his INR was stable for the third week in a row and he felt sharper, stronger and more rested than for months. He was walking further and thoroughly enjoying exploring his historic local town.

This week should also be the week that he was due for the all-clear from the cardiac team as long as he got an appointment through, although they were a little bit late in doing that.

His mood was in the stratosphere. He was almost dribbling with excitement.

He wasn't alone, either. Veda had spent a weekend fishing with his son and was starting to think about returning to work, Kelvin was settling well into a rehab programme and Clark was already back at work, acting as the chauffeur for his team around their many pest control missions.

Alas he elated too soon.

The following day he was informed that the atrial flutter was not responding as hoped, so he would need cardioversion treatment to shock it back into rhythm. When it came to it, it would be a quick procedure, over in literally seconds.

A cardioversion had always been a possibility, so he wasn't too surprised. In fact he was almost looking forward to it. He could pretend to be in a film where the heroine demands that people "Step away" before blasting him back to life with a single powerful charge. When would it be done? This week or next?

"It depends," he was told. "There's usually an eight week waiting list, and the lady who sorts it all out it may be on holiday. Of course you're not on it yet because we were hoping the flutter would sort itself out naturally. Unfortunately, it hasn't."

"OK. I'll put up with that. Can I fly? There's a good chance it will be essential for the next bit of work I get involved in."

"We don't recommend it."

His face, jaw, spirit and soul all dropped.

Can't fly? Another eight weeks? And that would only be after his name had been added to the waiting list.

This was horrendous.

It would add even more on to the time before he could be fully back at work. He feared that this could have some very unpleasant repercussions.

As a self-employed person no work meant no income.

No show, no dough.

Not a mantra.

A fact.

It seemed so cruel after the romping progress of the last two weeks. It confirmed to him that he was still in a fragile state. Certainly a lot more than he had begun to think over the last couple of weeks.

His mood plummeted.

Chapter 15 – The Vagaries Of Hope

"My mom always said life was like a box of chocolates. You never know what you're gonna get." Forrest Gump

Feeling alert made a huge difference. He had felt enthusiastic, energised and lively until that news about the potentially long wait for a cardioversion.

He had read somewhere that at about week eight the heart should be recovering from the operation itself, so patients could start gentle exercise. Apparently he could think about starting things like gentle jogging, cycling and non-contact sports. At least that was something to look forward to next week.

Meanwhile he worked off the frustration of the news about the wait for the cardioversion by walking even further than any day before. It was the one thing that was under his control and that he knew was doing him good. The stitches inside his heart should have dissolved by now and his sternum had stopped that strange grinding so was presumably knitting together satisfactorily. He felt he was doing pretty well overall and the previous weekend had even felt comfortable enough to socialise and move among small groups.

No more feeling mentally too slow to be able to contribute; no more obvious fear of getting an accidental knock in the chest.

There was always some way to find a positive.

At first it had been hard to accept that he wouldn't be fully recovered in six weeks because that had sounded like a crazily long time. Yet Charlie had been right and would probably be right about the twelve week mark, too. Having some semi-reliable timescales gave Ben some reassurance, even if he wasn't too happy with them.

Up to this point it had been about survival and getting back on his feet. Now he could realistically start to plan ahead and think of the twelve week mark as a point that he felt he could comfortably be back at work and, more importantly, back in control of his own life and time. His concentration was noticeably sharper and his walking was getting more and more powerful. At times he was even starting to accelerate for short bursts.

Now he could lie on his side and his front, which meant he could sleep in comfort and twist to give Jamie a cuddle. He could push up from a chair to a standing position. He even felt confident to increase the weights he could move around or lift.

He started trotting very short distances. It wasn't exactly the 10k he had loftily promised himself at the start, but to run even twenty metres was liberating and yet another sign that he was improving. He got a real buzz when he ran the two hundred metres to the post he had taken so long to walk to on his first day home.

He was improving although still didn't know whether it was a reasonable rate of improvement or not. He could do with it being confirmed.

Week seven started well. His close friend and main point of contact at work visited to discuss work packages with the offer to "do whatever you want. Just come back." It was perfectly timed vote of confidence as a little boredom was starting to nudge into his days. He felt mentally prepared and they agreed he would start again part time the following week.

All he needed for his own assurance was the all-clear from Massimo's team.

Since coming home he had been putting a lot of store on this appointment.

This was to be the sign-off from the cardiac surgery team and he expected to be told that his recovery was on track and that his sternum was knitting well enough for him to be able to drive safely. He didn't want to presume or work that out, though. He wanted to be told it, face to face, by a specialist who knew about these things.

If he had permission to drive, a full return to work was realistic and he would also be able to travel further afield than his local town, magnificent though that was. And the more disappointments he got from being part of the Process, the more store he placed on this freedom.

So he was furious when the appointment came through with almost another two weeks to wait.

The appointment to see Massimo two weeks after leaving hospital – a key condition of his discharge – hadn't materialised at all. So he had no idea if he was progressing reasonably or not.

Hope raised then dashed yet again.

The same day he had a long scheduled appointment with his local surgery to review his progress and hopefully to gather some guidance on things to concentrate on as well as getting an idea of whether his progress was good, bad or ugly.

What a frustrating and rage-inducing waste of time.

He was left to discuss his case and progress with a complete stranger who didn't know who he was or what had happened. And to make it worse, who hadn't even bothered to skim through his notes.

For Ben, this was a massive week. He wanted to know things like, could he exercise? If so, how hard? How was he doing in comparison with others? Was he average? Above average? Below? Any comments about the atrial flutter and the right-side heart failure, the complications that had developed as a consequence of the operation?

All he got was "It depends," "Take it slowly," or "I can't see it on your notes." The GP didn't quite say "What's INR?" but Ben felt he may as well have done so. No mention whatsoever of those complications that Ben thought could easily be causing him invisible problems.

He felt undervalued and disrespected.

It was as if the message was 'if we don't tell you there's something wrong then you should presume everything is fine. Don't bother us.'

It was as if positive affirmation was a fool's paradise when in his professional world it was basic common sense. This approach really, really didn't work for Ben.

It had taken seven months of worry to find out there was something wrong in the first case and another four months to actually do anything about it; and all the time his heart condition had been deteriorating. Yet nobody would tell him what he either could or should do now.

He was boiling with anger when he left the room.

"What else am I not being told?"

The following day he got a note informing him that he was on a waiting list. No mention of which one, where it was for, or how long he should typically expect to wait. He was just on a waiting list. He felt despair. He was back in the Process and he was therefore subject to its rhythms and timelines, and poor old Jamie felt the full force of his sadness.

Could this week get any worse?

Oh, yes.

Chapter 16 – Another way

"I can't change the direction of the wind but I can adjust my sails to reach my destination."
Jimmy Dean

Mid-way through week eight ATO he got a call from the local cardio rehab team: there's space in a course to start in eight weeks' time. Would he like to join it?

"What's involved?"

"One two-hour group session per week over ten weeks. The first hour is discussion about how you feel and some education, then an hour of exercise where you do as much or as little as you feel like."

They used a 'how it feels for you' scale to determine the intensity of any exercise and they were keen for him to know that he could stop at any point he wanted to. In some cases that may mean only doing anything to the extent that you can carry on a conversation; other times it could mean building up a bit of a sweat and pushing as hard as you feel.

But nobody would tell him how hard that could or should be. "It all depends on how you feel," she said.

That was too vague. He felt it could only reinforce any unwillingness or laziness. He firmly believed he needed to be pushed much harder if his heart was to get better.

"So that would be fifteen weeks after the operation before it started? And it's a ten week course on top of that?" That would have serious implications for his availability to work.

How could he not sign up? If he rejected a rehab programme then he was hardly doing everything he could to improve. So he signed up and said he would wait for further information in due course.

When he came off the call he felt cross. He would probably have been even more annoyed had he known that by this time Kelvin was already in the third week of a similar course in a different part of the country. He would have finished his before this one even started.

Ben usually felt a small tinge of guilt when railing against the Process. After all, the same Process had saved his life so it felt a bit churlish to complain about having to wait a few short weeks.

Now, however, he felt he was in a real life game of snakes and ladders and it wasn't funny. Every big stride forward of the last few weeks felt as if they had been wiped out by this week's news.

Now the plan of eight to nine weeks fully back at work was obliterated. That was disappointing, although in itself it wasn't a problem. It happens. Plans change. The issue was that there was no end in sight.

Stress came back in a big way. He was deflated and almost defeated. Crikey, this was even affecting his mindset. Not good by any measure.

As usual, it was the not knowing that was hurting.

That evening Jamie tentatively suggested they try a different approach.

There was a private hospital in a nearby town and she had quietly identified a cardiologist who seemed to have a good reputation and who appeared to prefer a preventative approach to heart health, using a combination of good nutrition and exercise. Ben could get to see him quickly.

The downside was that the cost would probably completely wipe out what savings they had, which meant that the longer Ben had to stay off work, the more debt they would accumulate. It was a dilemma. To wait and hope or take the chance?

They decided to at least find out what the cost could be and invested in a provisional consultancy with Doctor Xavier, a consultant who was an interventional cardiologist. Amazingly, they could have a full hour's appointment in just two days' time.

It was well worth it. At the appointment, Ben instantly felt comfortable.

Xavier listened attentively to his version of the story then quickly read the copies of letters they had received and fed it back as he understood it so far. He translated it into a language and described events in a way that Ben could understand and relate to.

To add to the hope, Jamie said that she thought Ben's heart may have returned to normal rhythm. She had been finding it difficult to lay her head on his shoulder as it wasn't very relaxing listening to the irregular beat of the flutter. This morning had been different. The steady, rhythmic beat sounded exciting.

Could it mean something?

One of the options now open to Ben was that he could have the cardioversion performed through this clinic within a couple of weeks.

After Jamie mentioned that she thought Ben's heart may have returned to normal rhythm, Xavier checked and said that the pulse did indeed seem to be steady. They could book an ECG in this hospital to confirm it, if they wished. That would tell them whether the cardioversion was actually necessary or not.

All of a sudden Ben had a realistic choice. No more waiting or wondering. Instead he could choose a set date. It would put them back in control.

Admittedly, it would wipe out their remaining savings, but it offered the possibility of regaining control over his life and getting back to earning a living once more. Ben would be able to give work some realistic dates and plan around those rather than having to wait for his turn to be determined by the Process. It would take all of the doubt and uncertainty out of the equation.

And this guy actually spoke to him. Looked him in the eye and gave his opinion, for better or worse. He didn't hold back. What a difference.

Xavier mentioned an associated rehab programme that members of his team were developing and in a perfect world Ben would follow that. Their approach is to work the heart as it is supposed to be worked: as hard as is safe for the individual.

All he had to do was meet the costs and all could be arranged to near enough suit his own times.

Hope had come bouncing back into Ben's life like an excited puppy. The session with Massimo's team was due next week, so they decided to wait for the outcome of that before finally making a decision about which way to go. But now there was a choice.

They were both very excited as they drove home. Far better to live in hope than frustration.

Chapter 17 – As You Were

*"We must accept finite disappointment, but
never lose infinite hope." Martin Luther King Jr*

What an up and down couple of weeks.

In week eight ATO Ben started back at work for three
half-day sessions, working from home. He didn't feel he
could drive just yet, although the delayed appointment
with Massimo and his team was due at the end of this
week. After the sudden release of the restraints the
previous week he hoped that this week would follow suit.

Theoretically he could drive after four weeks, by
which time the bone should be strong enough, but this
was a confidence matter. Anyway, he didn't honestly
trust the insurance company not to change their minds
even though they had verbally confirmed their policy.
Charlie came back into mind. "Don't rush it. It's not a long
time in the grand scheme of things."

He had anticipated that he would get straight back
into the swing of things at work, so was a little surprised
to find that mentally balancing the wide range of issues
and solutions was exhausting. It was great to be back. He

had badly missed his team mates. Yet it would clearly take more time to fully pick up the rhythm once again.

By eight weeks Clark had already been back at light work for three weeks and had been discharged from the cardiac surgery team at the hospital. All was progressing quite well and they felt he would be back to his best in three months.

In contrast, Veda had been instructed to stay away from work for an additional two months to give him more time to heal after his complicated operation.

Kelvin was of course almost halfway through his own rehab programme and his smile was growing wider with each passing day.

The day of reckoning arrived. He was due to see Massimo's team. He was excited.

This would be such an important session in so many ways, especially for his confidence and belief that what he had been doing was right. It would mark progress and he would be told if he was moving along as hoped.

Soon after arrival for the appointment, he was whisked away for an ECG and told the consultation would include a review of the results. At first glance the operator mentioned that it didn't look like there was any atrial flutter on the graph, although it was important that it was the consultant who decided that.

Ben got quite excited by the possibilities. Who knows, the news this afternoon could all be really good. Can't wait to be called now, although there were signs suggesting that appointments were running a bit late today. So he waited.

And waited...

And waited...

Two hours later the clinic was clearing and everybody seemed to be heading home. Ben had been forgotten about. His notes had either been misplaced or got mixed up with someone else's. The error was identified when an unattached ECG chart and a lonely patient turned up at the end of the shift. By that time, all of Massimo's team had left, so staff scurried around trying to find someone who could stand in.

Ben's discharge was eventually performed by an on-call doctor who was dragged off the Cardiology HDU.

In between calls in response to his bleeper, the doctor tapped Ben's breast bone a couple of times and said that there didn't seem to be a problem. When Ben asked if he was OK to drive now, he reluctantly said that he wouldn't say he couldn't. "Any other questions?" as his bleeper rang for the fifth time.

He was doing his best to answer the questions, but on call means on call for emergencies and he couldn't just ignore it. The poor man had been put in an impossible position and was trying, and failing, to balance two conflicting demands on him.

Ben was devastated and it showed. He began a bitter and angry tirade. Couldn't they see that this really mattered to him? He was here to be informed, not left to guess what on earth they could mean by avoiding a question with a double negative and a load of medical terminology. He had come here anticipating a massively significant personal announcement and instead what he got was a standard set of guesses from a doctor who had been dragged off the wards and who had never seen his notes or any results other than that damned ECG he held in his hand.

He was so desperately upset he was almost crying. All that hope and anticipation, all those worries that were to be silenced in this meeting. He was still just another lump of flesh to this lot. It was only Ben and his immediate family who ever thought that he mattered at all.

Fortunately Ben realised before the red mist took over completely that it was futile getting upset at this man. "Be reasonable, Ben. He had been good enough to step in to fill the gap caused by another person's errors. He wasn't the one who had caused it. Ease off, you idiot."

He apologised to the doctor for his reaction and thanked him for taking the time out to help. He would presume that he was now OK to drive and that his chest was probably knitting together in line with most other people because he hadn't told him it wasn't. The doctor wouldn't disagree.

The afternoon had been very frustrating but it wasn't the doctor's fault. In the light of day it would come out as a simple administrative oversight. "Sheesh, look what I did Sheila. I picked up two sets of notes at the same time. Silly me!" someone would say tomorrow, before forgetting all about it.

Except it had happened on the day that Ben had been getting worked up about through eight weeks of emotional turmoil. Jamie looked at him sorrowfully. She knew exactly how he was feeling because she felt the same: badly let down.

He left the building, so furious and disappointed that he couldn't speak sanely. He now understood more than ever the phrase 'It's the hope that kills you'.

He had to find a positive from this. At least he probably had permission to drive. Or that's what he guessed he was supposed to take from that double negative. So he got in the driver's seat and drove home for the first time in eight weeks.

Carefully.

Lost in the fury were the results of the ECG. It more than suggested that the flutter had gone. In the midst of the bleeper calls, the good doctor had said that there was absolutely no trace of it in the printout. If that was true then it really would be good news.

On the drive back home they rapidly concluded that taking up Xavier's proposal was another no-brainer decision. They would find a way to pay. Then they got lucky again. A battery of tests at the clinic and a further hour's consultation with Xavier could be made available for two days' time.

The emotional swingometer careered in the opposite direction. Maybe these tests would bring better news.

Two days later, within the space of three hours, Ben had an ECG, an echocardiogram and a full consultation. Xavier had found a way to look at all of Ben's notes so had a comprehensive bundle of information to discuss and could identify any trends. It was helped when Ben gave him a copy of the ECG from two days earlier.

Xavier provided a full and skilled interpretation of what had gone on so far and what Ben should expect to come, even when it meant there could be bad news ahead. Yes, there was some functional impairment in the other side of the heart; but that wasn't unusual. On the face of it, it appeared to be responding reasonably well and that was encouraging. The operation itself looked like it had been a roaring success and his valve was working well with only minimal leakage; again, many people experience that so it's not unusual.

He took the time to look Ben and Jamie in their eyes and talk to them. He explained what the realistic options were. Importantly, he told Ben what he could and shouldn't do yet. He even ventured an estimate of when he could expect to do things, presuming his recovery stayed on track. He also told him that he should be safe to come off two of his tablets, the Warfarin and a heart rate control drug, in a month's time as long as everything progressed as expected and his INR stayed in range for the next 28 days.

Ben's confidence soared. He trusted this guy. Why wasn't everybody like this?

Xavier had achieved inside three hours what Ben had been trying to get for the last six weeks to no avail. Yet all he had really done was to also say "It depends." Except Xavier had spoken with Ben and not at him or to 'the patient'. The difference was incredible.

There was even better news.

The ECG from that afternoon confirmed that his atrial flutter had righted itself. There would be no need for the cardioversion now, no need to sit on a waiting list and he was OK to fly. He could go back to work.

Life was back on the up. From pits to the peaks inside a three day period. Wow. What a joyride.

He hadn't even noticed that Xavier had been calling him Benedict all this time.

Chapter 18 – Taking Back Control

"I am not what happened to me. I am what I choose to become." Carl Gustav Jung

Talk to a good wellness coach about health in general and she or he will soon be explaining that a person's health is affected by everything going on and that has gone on in their lives. Among other things it helps to explain why two people who experience exactly the same set of conditions can have massively differing reactions. It all depends, you see.

To add to this roller-coaster of hope and despair around the reporting on his recovery, Ben had his fair share of events going on in his life at that time.

Two months before his operation his mother had passed away after a long struggle with dementia; while he was in hospital his beloved sister-in-law had suddenly and tragically died after a short and vicious illness; days after that an aged aunt passed away. Then three weeks after that event, Chris, a tough teammate from his sports playing days, also died suddenly from an aortic aneurism. The question of his own mortality was unavoidable.

The day after Chris' funeral, Ben turned sixty. Turning sixty was a life event that he had been dreading. Some people embraced it, others withered with it. For his whole life he had looked at it as the age that people officially become old. He really wasn't up for that. He was still only thirty three and at the peak of his powers, wasn't that obvious?

It was ten weeks ATO to the day.

While he cradled a celebratory glass of wine he thought long and hard about things, searching for reasons to feel sorry for himself.

"Don't be such an egotistical idiot," he concluded and instead determined to use these events to help him keep his own issues in perspective. Yes, his situation was serious, and at one stage was potentially terminal. Now it wasn't. It had been fixed, the underlying gear was in reasonable condition as shown by the angiogram and he now no longer needed cardioversion. He also had a family who had bent over backwards to accommodate and support him.

"Count your blessings and appreciate your luck."

It was another a pivotal moment.

That realisation provided him with a source of strength when times got difficult in the weeks that followed. He no longer needed to rely on murmuring "This too shall pass" in dark moments.

Instead all he needed to do was to snarl at himself like Mr. T. "Perspective, fool."

There were things he could do to claw back control.

The obvious one was to invest in the rehab programme that Xavier had recommended. It suggested all sorts of benefits and, probably most importantly, it would be him and only him in the session. He would be getting personal attention and all of the work would be dedicated to getting him and his heart back up to speed as efficiently as possible. He would no longer have to wait as the Process slowly unfurled.

He was taking positive steps forward, rather than having to wait for an event to happen before he could move. He was excited again, which he reckoned could only be doing his body good as the feel-good chemicals flowed. Yes, there were frustrations and there would doubtless be more because that's the way life works.

He felt he was taking control again and it energised him. He and Jamie started to get excited.

So it was that eleven weeks after his operation, Ben began his rehabilitation programme.

No longer would he have to be happy with lots of walking and some stretching or gentle jogging each day. This was to be an intense programme of two hours per week for each of ten weeks, supplemented by 'homework'. The three person team of specialists included two cardio specialists who were also qualified personal trainers, and an international athletics coach. Their brief was to encourage the recovery of Ben's heart so that he could engage in life confidently again. Or, as he measured it himself, to get him back to where he had been fifteen months earlier.

Ben was a bit nervous. He really didn't fancy the idea of repeating the previous twelve weeks and, while exercising, was very conscious of the fact that he was holding something back. Just in case.

Unwittingly he had allowed his posture to roll inwards as if to throw a protective bubble around his heart and sternum. His shoulders and spine had become rounded, encouraging his head to bow forward and he had taken to carrying something – anything – in front of his chest whenever he went anywhere. His body language screamed out that he was still in protection mode.

Sorting that out was a challenge to take on.

 When he arrived for his first session, he was full of trepidation. That could only be eased by actually doing something. He forced himself to go through the door.

It was chaotic. Yet he absolutely loved it. He was immediately pushed further than he had dared to think about while he was marching around town under his own steam. He was absolutely delighted.

Each session was in two distinct parts. He spent the first half hour on a static bike, wired up to a heart monitor to precisely record his performance. The second involved exercises designed to loosen then strengthen his muscles, with particular early focus on releasing his back and shoulders.

Being monitored so closely was a whole new experience that Ben found both fascinating and exhausting. He was quickly shown how to ride a bike "like the professionals but at about half their speed," and was introduced to the relevance of his power output, wattage, cadence and heart rate. Distance covered and speed were irrelevant. It wasn't simply a case of blasting away as fast as he could for a while and stopping when he got too tired. No, this was much more scientific.

The key was to steadily build up to a point of high and sustained effort before gently being brought down to a lower heart rate. That way the heart was actually protected and strengthened at the same time. He was told that a sudden stop would cause the heart to work harder and more explosively than if it slowed down gradually. That would not be a good idea and he should avoid doing that. "Even walking up a hill," he was told, "don't simply stop and get your breath back. Far better for your heart to keep moving at a slower pace."

He still had some doubts, though. Every medic he had spoken to up to now had cautioned him to be careful, to take things slowly and to stop if he felt breathless. While he intuitively felt that was only encouraging his body and mind to work at a constantly reducing rate, which would end up with him less fit than before, there was such commonality of the message that surely they were all right?

It was akin to telling pain patients to 'let pain be your guide and stop just as it arrives'. It was obvious to Ben that would mean the patient would anticipate pain earlier and so bit by bit stop doing any exercise at all.

"No. The heart is a muscle. It needs to be worked," they would say. "It can't improve if you don't work it."

At the beginning of each session they took a set of measures, to monitor any progress he managed to make. That in itself opened a whole new world to him. Measures that he had previously viewed as either expensive to attain or relevant only for doctors reports, suddenly took on a meaning of their own.

Apart from the usual weight and blood pressure measurements, now his waist size, body fat, muscle mass and visceral fat percentages all became relevant. He was shown what they all represented and why they were important. Even better, he had some standard numbers to work towards. No more guessing. He was either inside a guideline or outside. That's much better. He had a structure to work with and could set himself some realistic targets to work towards. Now he would know if he was progressing or not, which made his satisfaction independent of the Process.

It was an absolutely ideal setup for him and he flung himself into it with delight.

Chapter 19 – Back To Good

"The heart is a very, very resilient little muscle. It really is." Woody Allen

Charlie had been right again. "You'll feel ready to start to fire on all cylinders after about twelve weeks." Twelve weeks ATO he felt ready.

He felt as positive as he had felt in a year. He was walking and getting out in the fresh air every day, socialising, driving and all in all having a good time. He was also fully back in the swing of work and earning money to restore the savings he had used up. He sensed he was moving through finer definitions of recovery. He wasn't quite as fit as he was a year before so didn't feel he had 'recovered' yet, although he genuinely felt that was just a matter of time. And he had started a fully personal, scientifically measured rehab programme with three specialists, supported by the trusted Xavier.

Twelve months ago no matter how hard he worked, his fitness was going backwards. Now he felt that any exercise he did was adding to his improved fitness rather than merely slowing the rate of decline. The psychological and emotional difference it made was immense. This was a way forward.

Now he wanted to know how far he could realistically push and how to speed up the process.

At twelve weeks his breast bone should have fully knitted together, yet he still couldn't make himself beat his chest even in fun, he couldn't think of doing a press-up without a mental image of the long-healed stitches in his heart ripping open, and the constant stiffness in his back was an ogre that still haunted him every day.

Carla, the rehab team lead, assured him it would be impossible for him to hit his chest hard enough to damage it. It was elementary mechanics. There simply wasn't enough leverage to get up the momentum or power. Nonetheless, he still didn't do a Tarzan for another two weeks and only after a regular set of exercises dedicated to stretching the skin. Even then the eleven year old in him felt very brave.

It is safe to say that the sessions weren't concerned about working at 'moderate' intensity by any definition. These were intensive and Ben could feel his body responding and getting stronger as the weeks rolled by.

"The heart is a muscle. It needs to be worked," they would say. "It can't get stronger if you don't work it."

He asked what would happen if he pushed too hard.

"You won't," he was told. "Your legs would give out first followed by your lungs. Your body would give up on you long before your heart. And even if you did keel over, you couldn't really be with better people to sort you out immediately, could you?"

Everything about the programme was fascinating and provided a focus for him. He was seeing the body and how it functioned in a wholly new way.

He was learning again and he loved it. Each week he would attend the two sessions and complement them with additional exercise on his own. He was moving forward both physically and mentally at an increasing pace mainly thanks to the simple matter of somebody paying him attention.

After taking the tests and consultations with Xavier, Ben had adjusted his plan. He would focus on getting physically stronger for ten or twelve weeks and then add in changes to his nutrition after that. He was happy that the gym-based sessions focused on his exercise and mobility rather than nutrition. He didn't fancy that extra pressure just yet. He was enjoying himself.

Meanwhile in other regions, by the time of Ben's second session, Kelvin was already eight weeks into his own area's rehab programme, Veda was still patiently waiting for his body to settle down and Clark was still waiting to be told what he could or couldn't do.

And potty mouth Flo was sat at the back of her own first cardiac rehab session, raging at a condescending lecturer and her inability to distinguish between a keen, exercise focused woman who was desperate to get back to fitness and the 80 year olds who really didn't want to be there at all.

Nutrition-wise, Ben was fairly content with what he put into his body nowadays so he wasn't too concerned. It was a mix of fresh food, and only occasional fries, sweets or cookies. It was pretty good, although at times he admitted it could have been better. Especially his penchant for a drop of wine.

Anyway, he reasoned, his situation was about fixing a fault and not a result of a cardiac disease, so massive changes to lifestyle weren't a necessity.Yet..

Since the very start he had been asking three key questions and sensible nutrition was the number one answer to one of them. And he had ignored it!

What a dummy.

Not a mistake he would make if he ever had to experience the same again. Which would be, like, never, if he had his way.

Four weeks into the programme, Ben was stunned to be presented with a gift of a bike from his family. They also paid for a full set of accessories. Padded shorts to avoid saddle sores, bright lights to enable him to ride at night, a helmet and high visibility jacket. He passed on the possibility of specialist cycling kits. He was never going to allow himself to become a MAMIL – a Middle Aged Man In Lycra.

Having a bike introduced him to a whole new world. As well as providing an alternative way to exercise, he was now free to explore many times further than he could if only walking or trotting. He thrilled in taking full advantage of it.

He would take the bike to his lodgings when he was working away and spend the evenings touring the local countryside and estates in delight. When at home he discovered a previously unexplored local network of paths and cycleways to investigate.

Things were most certainly getting better.

By week 17 ATO, week six of the programme, the results were confirming that it was working and the stretching, loosening and mild resistance exercises were having a visible impact.

Time to up the game.

He was encouraged to do a full press-up.

To Carla and team it was just another exercise. To Ben, this was the most enormous event of the last two months. It represented a huge hurdle in his mind.

A mere six weeks ago he had been far too scared to even consider the thought of a press-up. Now he had clearly improved to a position where his coaches thought he could get down on all fours, perform a press-up and then stand up again. Six weeks ago that was physically and mentally impossible. Today they thought he should give it a go.

He completed not just one, but three then stood up, grinning widely.

The knowledge and feeling that his body could actually handle the pushing and pulling and various strains on the muscles involved in a press-up was psychologically immense. The idea of recovery was now in sight. It was no longer merely a dream.

His heart was still in normal rhythm, he had stopped two of his tablets two weeks earlier, he had the thrill of owning and using a bike and he was picking up new knowledge each week. Life felt very rosy indeed.

He knew this was a major turning point.

Now he was starting to actually heal. In his mind, 'recuperate' had probably ended at week six and now the 'repair' stage was over. Now he was healing. There's an enormous difference because healing involves the mind and belief.

His confidence and energy levels soared.

Thereafter there was a noticeable shift in his mindset. He was back to being in control of his actions and he felt that his body was strong enough to rise to any sensible demands he placed on it without any fear of post-operative damage.

Delays in appointments no longer mattered; he could answer to being called 'Benedict' and would even offer his date of birth without a huffy pause and a sarcastic intake of breath.

 Discuss the idea of healing with the very best wellness coaches and they may well come out with the idea that healing is significantly enabled by a combination of safety, creativity and connectivity. By now Ben had all three facets and they were powering him along in great surges.

He still wasn't as fit as he was before all of this started, but he could sense the day that would happen, and it would be in the foreseeable future, not months away. Disappointments were few and far between and mattered less. Even his hair and nails were growing again, which were both signs that the stress had gone. He was enjoying himself.

Towards the end of the programme he invested in a blood pressure monitor and a body composition monitor so he could continue to track the measures that he had become accustomed to. They weren't expensive. It had been fascinating to watch the numbers move - or not - over the weeks and he was interested in following them for the longer term.

The week after the end of the rehab programme he and Jamie went on a short holiday and after seven days of walking, cycling and ozone filled seaside air he finally felt as fit as he had done before it all began. And unlike before the operation, he also felt he could improve.

Two weeks after returning from the holiday, a colleague asked him how the recovery was going. Without thinking, he answered "What recovery?". He had temporarily forgotten that he had had a major operation just six months earlier. That spoke volumes.

He had hit his goal.

EPILOGUE

"We are healed from suffering only by experiencing it to the full." Marcel Proust

The practical result of the rehab programme was to give Ben and Jamie the confidence and permission for him to simply get on with things without worry.

He moved from feeling cautious and scared at the start of the programme to confident, optimistic and excited by the end.

There was no way he could put a price on that.

Six months after the operation he was feeling great. He had met his initial definition of 'recovery' and now started thinking in terms of improving his fitness. It was so encouraging to know that his fitness was back on an upward trajectory rather than in a downward spiral.

At seven months, he finally started to do what he should have done at the outset and pay some proper attention to his nutrition. He admitted that he had ignored and avoided it for the last year because he was concerned that he would invariably have to give up something that he enjoyed, which would only make him feel as if the whole nutrition and diet thing was being imposed on him. He also knew that meant he would probably drop it quickly. He didn't want to give anything up, especially as he was recovering from a fault rather than an illness.

The nutritionist was patient and followed his request to keep things as simple as possible.

"Here are three simple rules. Follow them and you are almost certain to see results. I can make it a lot more complex, but it's much more sustainable to give advice that is easy to follow.

One – Drink two litres of water per day. That's straightforward water. The likes of coffee, beer and sodas don't count in that total.

Two – Sleep eight hours per day.

Three – Cut the poisons. Replace processed foods with fresh foods, keep a close eye on the amount of sugar you eat, and ease off on the alcohol.

That's it."

"Is it honestly that simple?" he asked.

"Yes" she said.

And it was. Within four days he felt a difference. And there had been very little effort.

In the months following that meeting he felt cleaner, sharper and stronger than he had for years. Yes, there were times when he fell off the wagon but these three instructions were so simple that it was easy to climb back on board.

One year to the week after they were all freed from hospital, the Cardiac Crew met up again to share their stories of recovery.

It was a day of instant companionship and laughter. They compared scars by lifting their shirts like little children in a nursery then reminisced as if it had been the time of their lives.

The bypass lightweights observed to their mutual apparent joy that the legs where the blood vessel had been taken out were always slightly bigger than the other one. Like narcissistic prima donnas they then complained that the scars were a bit unsightly.

Kelvin looked at least twenty years younger. He was clearly a very happy man. He had started his rehab programme within four weeks of getting home and had evidently closely followed the instructions and nutrition advice he had been given. He now included long and regular walks as a daily enjoyment and he looked slim, fit and fresh faced and positively fizzed with energy.

He had actually gone straight from the hospital and started to lay small tiles. Fortunately, he soon realised that it was not a good idea so he asked his son-in-law to do the work for him while he concentrated on getting better. It obviously worked. He looked fantastic.

Veda too looked fabulously fit and happy. "Well, you just get on with it, don't you? I didn't have a plan. I just got on and did things as I felt better, didn't I?" The most notable thing he had done was to give up salt and he looked and felt incredible for it. His issues had been complex and he needed to make changes to his lifestyle. He had clearly done exactly that.

It had been five full months before he returned to work and now he was as busy if not busier than ever before. He was loving life and his whole face still changed when he talked about the peace he found in fishing and the fun he had working with his birds.

Clark had a different story to tell. He had gained and lost twenty kilograms over the year and a minor little accident when he knocked out his catheter had resulted in an ongoing urinary issue that was still getting attention. He had been discharged by the hospital's cardiac surgery team after six weeks but due to a bizarre series of circumstances he had only had his first cardiologist follow-up review two weeks before this gathering. To compound matters, he had been told that there was no record of a heart bypass on his records.

In the absence of any advice to the contrary, he had basically done very little for the first twelve weeks after he got home. When he did emerge, he had experienced panic attacks when he walked into the openness of the fields where he used to roam freely and train his birds. He had been provided with no rehabilitation opportunity, yet, like Veda, he had just got on with things. When it came down to it he looked perfectly fine and his heart was feeling good.

A year on, he was back at work and training his birds of prey because he had got bored and nobody had told him he couldn't. So he made himself do it. Smiling all the time, of course. He was delighted to have been given a second go at life and was going to enjoy every moment.

News came through of other ex-inmates.

Flo had spent a year in denial, although throughout had appreciated the family and family events more than ever before. She wasn't interested in missing any more key moments with either her immediate family or her recently born grandchildren.

"The best thing," she said, "is that I am now able to say 'No'. Previously whenever I was asked I would jump in to help. That's what you do, isn't it? Now I say 'No' if I don't want to. Time with my family is irreplaceable."

Bree had been released early, had a dramatic blue light return to hospital for a bit more attention, then her lifelong healthy lifestyle had carried her through and she was as steady as she had ever been. Like Kelvin's, her own rehab programme had started within four weeks of leaving hospital.

Unsurprisingly, nobody had heard from Bert. They looked in the corners wondering if he was sitting there, chuckling. They guessed that instead he was in his front garden, happy as can be with his beloved Elsie.

They did have one salutary reminder that it wasn't all straightforward. Dennis had headed off home as the others had, yet had ignored the warnings not to lift heavy loads in the early weeks. As a result a year later his chest hadn't healed properly and was still creaking and scraping. He now carried a drainage tube and bag with him all the time.

More proof of Charlie's wisdom.

Ben had returned to work after eight weeks, started a rehab programme after twelve and actually forgot he had been operated on after six months. He felt full of energy.

He had rebooked and completed his postponed holiday with Jamie. They had spent a lot of time walking and climbing and had a picture of himself standing on top of a mountain that has become symbolic of his recovery.

He was exactly half a kilogram lighter than the day he checked in for his operation.

Ben looked back over the previous year and recalled the three questions that he obsessed about at the start.

What should he expect?

Well, everything may look the same, yet everything will be different. It was a roller-coaster of highs and lows, surges and setbacks. He had to learn to ride them.

It had taken six weeks to recuperate, six more to mend and another twelve to recover with consistent and committed effort. Although he could technically drive after four weeks, he hadn't felt confident enough or sharp enough to do so safely.

He had been surprised that the fuzziness in his head had lasted for as long as six weeks. None of his little projects were ever touched, although he had a file full of photographs of completed Lego models.

He could start back at work after eight weeks, although a more physical role would really require twelve. And going back to work was very tiring.

He had learned an amazing amount about the heart and the body. To this day he is still astonished that the body produces its own electricity and that's what sparks the heart in the first case.

It was a time of learning – a joy to him.

The whole experience left him physically and mentally stronger, yet he felt as if there was a hairline crack somewhere in him. A weakness had been exposed. He knew now that he was breakable. Both he and Jamie were also acutely aware of their own mortality and recognised that one day one of them would pass away and the other would have to live on.

That brought with it a small and significant psychological impact and introduced an extra caution whenever he looked to do something new. That made him uncomfortable, although he accepted that he would need to learn to live with it. From now on, his life would be different.

Conversely, he and Jamie found that the experience had encouraged them both to try activities they may never have previously entertained. They were certainly appreciating the full wonder of life a lot more.

What could he do to make a recovery quicker?

Number one should have been to attend to his nutrition and review how he fuelled himself properly. It makes an amazing difference and it's never too late or too early to start. He started late.

Get as fit and flexible as possible for when you go in. It will help when you go out, as Bree demonstrated.

Once in hospital, think "this too shall pass", practice patience and, to borrow the name of a quite brilliant book, 'Don't Sweat The Small Stuff', as it really is mostly small stuff. An obvious example was his name and date of birth. He had allowed it to bother him, and it had added so much stress to him and everybody around him that it was ridiculous. They really don't matter do they?

Don't rush it. Start slowly, set yourself targets then work hard and consistently towards them. Persistence and consistency are key. Oh, and invest in a back massager and get hold of a recliner for a few weeks.

And when someone tells you not to lift a load – listen to them. Ask Dennis if in doubt.

And how long would he be out of action for?

That's the "how long is a piece of string?" question. He made seven recoveries that he could identify. The Magnificent Seven, he called them.

- **One** was after ten days when he was deemed safe to leave hospital
- **Two** was on six weeks when his head felt clear and his body felt alive. The 'recuperation' was over. He could drive after four weeks, although he hadn't felt ready by that time.

- **Three** was on eight weeks when he started back at work. A significant moment.
- **Four** was on twelve weeks when he felt the 'repair' was over and he was ready to move on to getting fit again. When he started to heal.
- **Five** was the real one. On six months he felt as fit and strong as he had done when the little plumbing issue had first been observed and he temporarily forgot about the operation. This was his own definition of 'Recovery' from the outset.
- **Six** was a symbolic moment on ten months ATO having walked to the top of yet another tall mountain in New Zealand. He appreciated the irony that it happened to look down on Mount Doom, made famous in the Lord of the Rings films.
- **Seven** came almost four weeks after the Cardiac Crew had met up and thirteen months to the day ATO. He was told he could come off the final prescription tablet. What a feeling that was.

So how do you recover from open heart surgery?
Well, it depends…

Acknowledgements

To the Cardiac Crew and the amazing clinical and nursing staff who got me through this.

And to those kind souls who read through the early versions and provided constructive and extremely valuable feedback. Reading the originals in comparison to the final version was truly eye-opening.

And of course to my wonderful wife and family who looked after me so patiently.

Thank you so much.

Reading Group Discussion

Sometimes in a Reading Group it can be difficult to know where to start conversation. Try these suggestions:

- Do you personally know of anybody who has been through a procedure like this?
- Were Ben's questions clearly stated?
- Did he get adequate answers?
- The vast majority of patients had men's names. Do you think this story could also apply to women?
- Was Charlie a woman or a man?
- Was the book comforting or disturbing?
- Was the story encouraging or alarming?
- Who was the real star of this story?
- What do you think of the care they all received? Good, Bad or Ugly?
- Is excellence in healthcare reactive or preventative?
- What did you think of the writing style?

The story was written with plenty of short, sharp sentences and deliberately played a bit loose with the stricter rules of pure English grammar.

I hope you have some interesting discussions and would love to hear about them.

Contact details are on the final page.

If you enjoyed this book, please leave a review on the site where you bought it. And of course please feel free to spread the word and tell your friends to read it too!

Also by Steve Corkhill

Reboot For The Worn Out

Professional

More and more people in every country of the world are running into the challenge of burn-out. The novel yet proven technique of a personal Reboot offers a powerful and natural solution to these concerns.

'Reboot for The Worn Out Professional' was written for people who feel they are in a hole of some sort and want to get up and moving again – quickly. It's all about restoring the buzz and excitement, and providing a firm feel-good foundation on which to build the next phase.

The reboot is made up of a set of three simple steps following the analogy of a computer system reboot. It clears out the rubbish then provides a toolkit using some of the world's most effective and proven techniques for reviving the joie de vivre, most of which are free to use. If you like the idea of getting maximum output with as little input or disruption as you can, using mainly existing skills, having fun and trying something fresh along the way, then this is for you.

"You may not be responsible for being down, but you must be responsible for getting up." —Jesse Jackson

For a free sample of the book please visit
www.rebootforthewornoutprofessional.com

More books by Steve Corkhill

Using the pen-name of Barney Hegarty, Steve compiled
The Laugh Out Loud emails series

- The Art Of Miscommunication - Announcers and Help Desks
- The Art Of Miscommunication - Letters, Forms and Replies
- The Art Of Miscommunication - Comebacks and Answers
- Battle Of The Sexes - The Joy Of Marriage
- Battle Of The Sexes - War Of The Worlds
- Battle Of The Sexes - Men On Mars And Venus
- Battle Of The Sexes - Women On Venus And Mars
- Battle Of The Sexes - Stereotypes
- Tales Of The Unexpected - True And Embarrassing
- Tales Of The Unexpected - Did I Know That?

About The Author

Steve Corkhill is a one-time schoolmaster who evolved into an independent change management consultant working with a range of business and social sectors around the world. He has had the pleasure of being an integral part of many hugely successful projects and programmes in his career as well as helping hundreds of former pupils to a solid start to their adult lives.

He loves his work and is now delighted to add 'author' to his list of achievements.

His passion in life is to help people to move from a state where they are feeling worn down or out of control to a place where they feel enthusiastic, energised and encouraged once again. Then they will be back in charge of their own performance.

At the time of writing Steve lives in the magnificent world heritage city of Bath, UK, from where he travels, enjoys his family and indulges in his various hobbies.

Connect with Steve

If pushed to capture it in a sentence, Steve would accept that the overarching theme of his work and career is to

"Get You Back To Good"

"How To Recover From Open Heart Surgery" is a personal and very specific example of this theme. It is a true story, over 95% factually accurate with only name changes and a handful of minor plot lines laced into the narrative to emphasise particular points.

"Reboot For The Worn Out Professional" is also aimed squarely at helping in this arena.

To connect with Steve use:

Twitter: https://twitter.com/SteveCorkhill

Facebook: https://www.facebook.com/steve.ftwop

Email: Steve.Corkhill@FTWOP.com

OR sign up on the website

www.ftwop.com

You can also use the full name

www.forthewornoutprofessional.com

Any details provided will never be shared with or sold to third parties, you can cancel all communications at any time and they will only be used to provide you with information relevant to helping to Get Back To Good

Printed in Great Britain
by Amazon

80074227R00108